PRAISE FOR
BODY BECOMING: A PATH TO OUR LIBERATION

"In *Body Becoming: A Path to Our Liberation*, Dr. Robyn Henderson-Espinoza does remarkable work in translating so many of the fears of marginalized folks directly related to how our bodies are perceived in wider society. Their focus on the complexity of presentation reveals a critical truth to readers who may be new to these conversations: that there is ultimately no way our bodies can be hidden from the bigotry that targets our existence. I cannot recommend this book enough. It is essential reading for anyone hoping to engage in a good-faith effort to dismantle systems of oppression."
—Charlotte Clymer, transgender activist,
military veteran, press secretary

"Robyn Henderson-Espinoza's *Body Becoming* is pure gift. The story and wisdom of this nonbinary, transgender, Latinx theologian on the autistic spectrum presses squarely into the center of what it means to be embodied. In *Body Becoming*, Henderson-Espinoza takes readers along on their journey to understand, accept, and embrace embodied living. We all need this book. And in the midst of the COVID pandemic, we are ready for it. Get this book."
—Lisa Sharon Harper, president and founder of Freedom Road
and author of *The Very Good Gospel and Fortune: How Race
Broke My Family and The World—and How to Repair It All*

"In *Body Becoming*, the wonderful Dr. Robyn Henderson-Espinoza leads people like me—people stuck in their heads—toward a fuller experience of personal embodiment with wisdom, intelligence, and candor. But more than that, Dr. Robyn shows us how everything—really, *everything*—is somehow linked to our relationship with bodies, both human and corporate, spiritual, political, and otherwise. To say this is a brilliant book about embodiment is underselling it. It's really a brilliant book about *everything*."

—Pete Holmes, comedian, host of *You Made It Weird*, and author of *Comedy Sex God*

"Robyn Henderson-Espinoza has written a brave, intellectually astute, and artistic book in *Body Becoming*. In a time when so much of theological exploration devalues the body and destroys it, Henderson-Espinoza takes seriously the word that we must have life and life in its fullness. It is theory. It is poetry. It is love. It is witness. Somehow Robyn has created theological beauty that has learned how to witness and celebrate and embrace and make whole. This book is more than a freedom journal or active theology—it is a prayer, a sermon, and a love note to so many people trying to get free."

—Danté Stewart, author of *Shoutin' in the Fire: An American Epistle*

"The disembodied nature of modern society offers both personal and societal peril. In *Body Becoming*, Dr. Robyn holds these two perspectives in balance, offering the reader a bridge from knowing their body to making room for everyone else to do the same. This book is both life-changing and world-changing at once."

—Mike McHargue, author of *Finding God in the Waves: How I Lost My Faith and Found It Again Through Science* and *You're a Miracle (and a Pain in the Ass): Embracing the Emotions, Habits, and Mystery That Made You You*

"Dr. Robyn Henderson-Espinoza's body is a vast terrain of storied longings, traumatic memories, and troubling tensions. You would think that they would want to do everything to get away from it, to renounce it. Instead, by embracing this intelligent territory, they redeem it from its significatory internment as a fait accompli, electing instead to think alongside Deleuzo-Guattarian philosophies, relational cosmologies, liberation theologies, and the soft secretions of their own compelling narratives of struggle and emergence to weave an account of the body that is simultaneously strange, emancipatory, and—yes—joyful. I might be so bold as to prophesy that by the time you are done reading Robyn's book, you'd walk past the mirror to look outside the window—just to catch a glimpse of your face."

—Bayo Akomolafe, executive director and chief curator of the Emergence Network and author of *These Wilds Beyond Our Fences: Letters to My Daughter on Humanity's Search for Home*

"*Body Becoming: A Path to Our Liberation* is an eye-opening, powerful book. In sharing honestly about their own understandings of their body and detailing the wisdoms and challenges they've encountered while blazing a new path toward embodiment, Dr. Robyn Henderson-Espinoza tracks, deconstructs, and reframes humanity's relationships with our bodies. Vulnerable, provocative, and freeing, *Body Becoming* will help you see your body like never before and will empower a deep connection with the living, breathing entity that is you."

—Matthew Paul Turner, #1 *New York Times* bestselling author of *What Is God Like?* and *When God Made You*

"Even before the Spanish mystic Teresa of Ávila reminded us that Christ has no body on earth but ours, embodiment has been a core reality of Christian spirituality—but it's confounding how many forces conspire to keep us alienated from our own bodies and from each other's. Robyn Henderson-Espinoza writes vulnerably and powerfully to invite us all to make the necessary reconnections with our bodies, with one another, with God, so that we may truly embody justice, freedom, and democracy. Their vision is a vision of hope, truth, healing, and love. Read this book, and join the revolution!"

—Carl McColman, author of *The Big Book of Christian Mysticism: The Essential Guide to Contemplative Spirituality* and *Eternal Heart: The Mystical Path to a Joyful Life*

"In *Body Becoming*, Dr. Robyn Henderson-Espinoza invites you into a rich conversation about bodies. Robyn's reflections on a lifetime of embodied becoming will stimulate you to reconsider your relationship to your human body, and to the social relationships into which our human bodies plunge us as part of the body politic. Some books give you vital information. Some ask important questions. Some help you see from a new perspective. This book offers all of the above, plus this: it invites you to feel in your body your interconnection with all the bodies, human and otherwise, in which we live, move, and have our being. A beautiful book from a beautiful human being."

—Brian D. McLaren, author of *Faith after Doubt: Why Your Beliefs Stopped Working and What to Do about It*

BODY
BECOMING

A PATH TO OUR LIBERATION

ROBYN HENDERSON-ESPINOZA, PHD

Broadleaf Books
Minneapolis

BODY BECOMING
A Path to Our Liberation

Scripture quotations are from New Revised Standard Version Bible, copyright © 1989 National Council of the Churches of Christ in the United States of America. Used by permission. All rights reserved worldwide.

Published in association with Cathleen Falsani, www.sinnersandsaints consulting.com.

Print ISBN: 978-1-5064-7357-4
eBook ISBN: 978-1-5064-7358-1

To every body who is awakening in these moments of catastrophe, confusion, and chaos, and to every body that has endured catastrophe, confusion, and chaos. May we find one another in a new reflective light so that we sojourn the paths to our shared liberation. I am not free until we are all free. If that resonates with you, then this book is for you.

There exists 1,000 unbreakable links between each of us & everything else. The farthest star & the mud at our feet. . . . The pine tree, the leopard, the river & ourselves—we are at risk together, or on our way to a sustainable world together. We are each other's destiny.

—Mary Oliver

Democracy is the road to socialism. . . . The first step in the revolution by the working class is to raise the proletariat to the position of ruling class, to win the battle for democracy.

—Karl Marx

We are taught that the body is an ignorant animal [and that] intelligence dwells only in the head. But the body is smart. It does not discern between external stimuli and stimuli from the imagination. It reacts equally viscerally to events from the imagination as it does to real events.

—Gloria Anzaldúa

CONTENTS

CONTENTS

PRÓLOGO

When I first began to explore this book idea, my proposal to the publisher came from a deep place within my own interior life—my own developing relationship with my body, my own coming to grips with ways of being that were disembodied due to how I was socialized, my work in academia and church communities—while also meeting cultural biases toward the body. I wanted to lift up the messiness of the stories of bodies, including my own coming into my Trans body and how it felt so liberating.

By the time I sat down to write this book, we were living in a global health pandemic and facing a great amount of uncertainty around the existential threat to ourselves, our livelihoods, and so much more. My writing necessarily entered a new phase of its own becoming as the United States saw an acceleration of anti-Black racism, police violence, and incompetence on the federal level. I knew I had to write from an embodied place; from my own unstable standpoint that is working class (at times working poor), Queer, Trans, and Latinx; and from the life of an endless hustle to make ends meet and imagine the world I long to inhabit. The uncertainty of all that was emerging asked something of me, something specific and particular. The returning and repetitive question that swirled around in my mind and perhaps in my body was this: What are the conditions for embodiment, and who am I as a curious intellectual activist who longs for an embodied life?

What emerged after that year of writing is this book, which weaves together my own coming into my Trans body with a critical look at which bodies count in this country and why this is so—even as it seemed like the world itself entered into a new phase of its own becoming and in some ways its own embodying of radical difference. What I mean is that I was already in my Trans body before writing, but I was not embodying my Transness until I started to trace the landscape of my Transness and leaned into embodiment.

What you will find in this book are stories, recalled memories, and reflections informed by my own intimations of politicized theology, ethics, and imaginations for another possible democracy, all informed by my deep struggle and my hope against hopelessness. I write about my own complex history of violence and the ways trauma impacted me in material ways. I write as an exercise of imagining another possible world through a rearticulation of democracy, beginning, always, in the body. I didn't set out to write a book on democracy, but the more the United States began to reveal how precarious our current democracy is, the more I felt compelled to consider definitions of democracy and varying critiques of democracy within the field of political theory to help me rethink democracy. I also write as a theologian and as a storyteller who believes we have to imagine our own being rooted in our material bodies so that democracy can also be embodied rather than remaining an ecosystem of transactions.

This book also traces the contours of the philosophy of becoming, which has been central to my entire academic project and is something we can all learn to embody, if only we can get out of ideas we hold on to around mechanistic change. Becoming is rooted in relationality and asks us how a turn toward a generous and emergent relationality might accelerate processes of becoming that help us pivot out of mechanistic change and into a relationality that might actually save us. While I work to translate a lot of the philosophy of becoming and occasionally eclipse some aspects of becoming, in this book, I work to capture the central pieces to becoming related to bodies, my body, our bodies, our democratic bodies, and our collective bodies yearning for not only social healing but collective liberation. In the end, there is always more to say. But this book is a start. And points of departure are always important, as they nurture our roots.

When I take another look at these chapters now, I'm aware that a kind of formula emerges within these themes: bodies, becoming, motion, democracy. These four things may help us rethink our moment and cast a vision for another possible world. After all, it is the Zapatistas in Chiapas, Mexico, who inspired me to think about another possible world through their own ecosystem that is rooted in liberating themselves from capitalism and the Global North.

The four major themes of this book, listed as sections, are rupture, becoming, difference, and repetition. These four themes are inspired by the philosophy of Gilles Deleuze, a French postwar philosopher, and Félix Guattari, a French psychiatrist. They envisioned a philosophy and theories that overhauled continental philosophy, specifically the field of ontology, and their overhauling of philosophy impacts how we think, produce knowledge, and act in the world. When I discovered their work in my PhD program while living in Denver, Colorado, I was immediately drawn in, mesmerized by the way they wrote and collaborated with such skill. I sought out all the books they authored. They collaborated on many projects, working in community, and I found their work compelling. Their work helped me imagine another possible world through the lens of what I call the "politics of radical difference." My dissertation, on the materiality of the body, used the works of Deleuze and Guattari and the works of Gloria Anzaldúa. Each of these four themes can also be found in and throughout Anzaldúa's works, especially when she writes about her own body, the body of the borderlands, and the people who emerge from liminal space, which she theorizes as *nepantla*, a Nahuatl term that means "in-between" or "middle space." The inclusion of these four themes helps guide the book into deeper folds of becoming, more compelling versions of embodiment, and helps imagine what is truly possible with an embodied life. This book echoes much of what Ignacio Ellacuría wrote about being contemplative in the way of justice. I am thinking about a kind of embodied life that compels us all toward a life of contemplation for the sake of justice.

We live in a world that is deeply composed of motion—people move on a global scale and create and re-create borders—and as we come into contact with these folds of necessary change, we see how related bodies, becoming, motion, and democracy actually are. My hope is that this book extends into a somatic awareness that what it takes for another possible world is a deepened awareness of our individual and collective felt sense—a life together, if you will, a politics of being *en conjunto*, a term I heard frequently growing up in Texas. Being *en conjunto* is an orientation to(ward) togetherness. Conjoined in a life together, if you will, so that our hyperindividualized orientations don't catapult us into a wayward life. There is so much pain on a global scale right now, and we desperately need visions for another possible world. This is why it's important to lean into the process of becoming and develop a somatic—an embodied—practice so that we can actually be in relationship with ourselves and with the world around us. So many of us have lost our habitat to gentrification; we no longer can afford to own land or even a house and no longer hear soundscapes of birds singing in the morning nor hear the trees whistle as the branches sway in harmony. How can we be in relationship with ourselves and with one another when a scarcity mentality is our guiding light? After all, many of us are emerging after being quarantined for almost two years, having lived through a global health pandemic (that still continues as deadly variants emerge), watching from our mobile devices and our couches as the coronavirus ravished the entire world. There are other struggles that we are confronting in these moments that have been ongoing for centuries, like anti-Black racism, the war on the poor and working class, and how to love our neighbors south of the border who desperately need a place to call home but are not welcomed because of our militarized borders, along with refugees in the Middle East needing a place to call home after Babylon, our US empire, invaded their countries. Pain exists on a global scale, and we desperately need another possible world.

An emergence back into the world requires us to participate in its becoming and in its embodied difference. How might having an orientation to a somatic practice accelerate new visions for another possible world? If we don't do this work, we won't survive ourselves or our impossible world.

Not everyone's language is grounded in theories that inform theological, ethical, or sociopolitical realities, but I hope you will bring your own language to this exploration, understanding the specific articulation here, as I believe that all theology is ethics and every theology is meant to be lived out in material bodies; our movements, too, need to embody deep practices of theological and philosophical reflection

so that our movements are more than transactions for justice making and actually create conditions for embodied
practices of material folds of justice that deeply embody the
never-receding horizon of a just life. This book is a call for a
clarion life that is rooted in embodied awareness.

|
RUPTURE

Often when we talk about rupture, we speak about disconnection or breaks. In studying the philosophy of Gilles Deleuze and later Dr. Thomas Nail, I learned that a rupture can be a good thing. It can also be a bad thing with material effects.

It is, in fact, a thing in and of itself and something to pay attention to.

Rupture, in Deleuze and Guattari's theory of the rhizome, offers a way of understanding, a point of interpretation. A rhizome (or something rhizomatic) is nonhierarchical and multiple. It may be an idea, a system, or a set of points on a line. Because they are multiple and nonhierarchical, when there is a rupture, the rhizome may break, causing other ruptures that might break away and form another line or reconnect with an existing line. Think here of crabgrass and the ways in which it grows in a multiplicitous manner, with many breaks or ruptures throughout the grass. Crabgrass is also nonhierarchical and multiple.

A rupture, when viewed throughout our cultural body, is best seen in rhizomatic ways: police brutality splits the rhizome, makes a break of the line of cultural body through violence, and causes harm to individual bodies and to our cultural body. These ruptures, however, do have a hierarchy, with harm being the highest point that causes a great amount of breakage within the rhizome of society.

If we take the rhizome to be a model of society, where connections flourish and multiply, when a rupture is created in the case of police brutality or the murder of George Floyd, society is harmed, and our cultural rhizomatic body is broken, traumatized. We either learn how to create a new rhizomatic line that is grounded in social healing or rupture additional harmful hierarchies.

Ruptures. They can be either good or bad, and (not to place ruptures in a strict binary moral value of good or bad) the breaks we experience either benefit us or don't. Whenever we experience a rupture or a break, we are called to repair the break and internalize the change so that we can become whole and social healing can emerge on a collective scale. Rhizomes encourage collective thought and collective action. Ruptures demand collective thought and collective action. May our rhizomatic society lean into its collective will so that we can repair the ruptures that are harming the least of these and those who are historically most impacted.

WHAT IS A BODY?

I am curious about bodies. I'm curious how we got to where we are with our understanding of bodies. For me, I have been on a five-year journey developing a relationship with my body and further deepening my relationship with what is sensate and seeking understanding in what it means to participate in my own becoming (em)bodied. Obviously, I've been on a much longer journey with my body, but these last five years, I've intentionally committed to befriending my body—my NonBinary Transgender Latinx body. As my therapist has asked me, "How can you be your own best friend?"

When I started thinking about and feeling into the question *What is a body?* I looked to different sources for answers, beginning with the dictionary. I was surprised—but not entirely—that the dictionary perpetuates a kind of Cartesian dualism that has harmed us for centuries. Answering this question requires each of us to engage with our own material being while also connecting to others' material beings, albeit sometimes through difficult dynamics.

When we begin to take seriously the felt sense of the body and the relationships that come from that felt sense, we can reshape not only our own bodies but the bodies of our culture and, finally, our cultural body. Doing this sets in motion a generative relationality that can ultimately reshape our democracy. That is my hope as I share the following curiosities with you. Do you have similar curiosities when it comes to the body?

Body is a word that is familiar to each of us, but do we know what a body is? A body is "the main part of a plant or animal body especially as distinguished from limbs and head," according to the *Merriam-Webster Collegiate Dictionary*. This sums up a specific approach we take when we often talk about a body—as something that is familiar but is almost never talked about as an entity, which includes the head.

When I was in graduate school, I remember starting to research topics for my doctoral dissertation. I expressed my desire to research the body to one of my professors. Dr. Edward Phillip Antonio is brilliant, by all accounts. Born in Rhodesia, he can quote philosopher Ludwig Wittgenstein by chapter and verse, including footnotes. So when I began to research my topic, I immediately tried to make an appointment with Dr. Antonio. It took numerous emails to finally get a reply. That was the one thing that was super frustrating: he didn't reply to emails. Yet he is a thinker in this complex world, and I aspire to his capacity, so I over-looked this fact.

When I approached his office, I unclipped my messenger bag, which had a seat belt for a buckle. It was clunky, and I'm not exactly graceful—I've been told I take up a lot of space. (I admit, I wore my hair as tall as Texas when I could!) After I got settled in Edward's office, I was ready to dig deep into conversation. I almost always had a cup of coffee or a water bottle with me. We agreed that we would meet for an hour to an hour and a half each visit, so I did my best to keep whetting my whistle when we spoke. With all my enthusiasm, I let him know I wanted to research the body for my dissertation. "Philosophy of the Mind?" he quickly responded. Even now I don't know whether he was asking me if I wanted to research the mind, the inner world of the head—which in this discipline of analytic philosophy is distinctly disconnected from the body—or flipping the script on me and suggesting the body has a mind. I have only now come to think about the complexity of his four-word question to me and the possibility of flipping the script after many years of my seeking to have a relationship with my body. Like I mentioned before, he is brilliant in every way!

After that initial talk with Edward, I set out on a journey to understand what a body is. Even after writing so much on the subject, I feel as though I am still scratching the surface of what a body is. It seems as though the mining of the body and understanding the body are ever-expansive processes. For example, you might ask, What is the relationship between a body and being? In academic circles, *being* is often understood as the philosophy of ontology, and we can trace the ways that *being* has been stabilized throughout history and has impacted our language, religious practices, habits, and policies, especially in this country and other democratized governments, largely due to the influence of Plato and Aristotle. And if our bodies are our being, then there is a connection to this branch of philosophy. But how does that help us understand what a body *is*?

For my part, I'd like to think that motion and being are part of understanding what a body is, a new and Queer fold of thinking about bodies that continues to bubble up in me as I read philosophy and theory. But that conversation with Edward is where I go back to my initial questions about the body. I still fumble through my thoughts when thinking about the body, and I still fall short in the ever-expansive understanding of bodies, but I'm learning to trust that the stories (and not only the ideas) that have shaped me will also shape you, the reader, in a way that further contributes to our understanding of bodies and their becoming. That conversation with Edward was and is a point of departure for this book, for this articulation of bodies and becoming and nurturing our roots in relationship and in conversation helps us get a bit closer to a more perfect union.

This initial conversation with Edward set me on my journey and raised a series of questions about the body, about my body, and about what a body in motion can be, change into, and become. At the time, I had been reading a lot of critical spatial theory and theories of place and space and had been researching the body as space or place. But one day, after a full day of reading (my day off from Apple), I was alone at my house enjoying a mug of fresh India pale ale. I invested in a kegerator during my PhD program and always had a pony keg of a really great IPA so that I could have beer on tap. As I was drinking my IPA, I had a thought: *Does the body become?* I had been reading Gilles Deleuze, too, during this time, so his philosophy of becoming had been metabolizing in my mind and perhaps in my body as well. I began thinking about the body not just as "a body" but as "the body" and as a body becoming.

From the question *What is a body?* I asked another: *What is a becoming body?* What does it mean for the body to become? Could the body be something that is more than the material reality of flesh and bone, consciousness and affect? Could the body also be a social reality? A collective body that is composed of all bodies within a particular geographic location, maintaining their own genus, species, and kind?

What is a body? What is a body that becomes?

Since the IPA day of questions, I have come to learn that the body has wisdom. That each cell in the body is in a sense a mind in itself. That the body is our teacher, whether we like it or not, and most times I don't like that my body teaches me hard lessons! When I set out to research the body, I was not in touch with the wisdom of the body that I now understand as embodiment or the ways that the body is sensate wisdom—and in that sense "in motion."

My journey to come into close relationship with my body has been not only a reflection on my own gender transition but also a looking back into my body's history, to when, at age sixteen, I had a brain aneurysm. So Dr. Antonio's question related to mind and to the body was a question deep in complexity and relationship for me.

My body has always had the wisdom they have needed. When I recount what happened in 1993 when my brain had an acute intracranial hemorrhage and when I look at how my body healed from the medical community's response of invasive treatment, I am amazed at the resiliency of my body. As I've listened to other stories of those with brain injuries, I realize not everyone has the same story as I do. No body is the same. And each body has inherent wisdom.

When I think now of the current uprising in the United States in the middle of a global pandemic, the particular years I write in and through continue to show us how culture is shaped by particular bodies, by those in power, by those making policy decisions, and by those with a microphone, and I grow concerned, I grow an urgency to understand how we might shift culture so that every body benefits and can be connected to other bodies within a given culture.

The questions deepen. Am I / are we aware of the process of change and how our bodies becoming actually reflects that connection?

As I continued to research the body, I came to understand how disconnected our bodies are and how philosophies and theologies accelerate what is a really profound disconnection. When I say "our" bodies, I am reflecting on what I see and experience in our society.

Not everyone is aware of "our" bodies as bodies living and socialized in the church and academia, both perpetuating a radical sense of disconnectedness from the body politic and from our own bodies, from the felt sense of who and what we are.

Even as so many of us were making our survivability primary during the global health pandemic, I began to put pieces together about disconnection and my body and how my brain worked. Sometimes I think I'm so smart, I'm dumb. And by that I don't mean to be disparaging toward myself.

What I mean is that my brain works in ways frequently praised by the academy but infrequently praised by society. Even my own understanding of myself as NonBinary and Trans has continually presented challenges for folks wedded to the gender binary as a way of understanding the body and culture. And add to that what I learned as I wrote this book in the summer of 2020: I am on the autism spectrum. Formerly known as Asperger's, this is what I learned, this true thing for me and my body. I am still becoming.

In 2018, I traveled to Cuba with my comrade, Rev. Alba Onofrio. We had a meeting at the seminary in Matanzas. Around us were all sorts of social cues during the meeting and after that I missed. In the car ride back to the place we were staying, a lovely penthouse apartment in Havana, Cuba, overlooking the Caribbean, Alba said, "You might

look into how people with autism negotiate social space."
My response? I was offended! Me? Autism? So much
about my life that Alba has commented on over the years
has been right—from naming the ways I am disconnected
from my ethnic and cultural roots to the reality that my
brain is neurodivergent.

But that was a piece of wisdom I didn't pay much attention to beyond taking offense, until several years later when
in a "relationship talk" with my partner, Erin. We had been
trying to figure out how to steward our relationship in a way
that makes us both feel amazing—isn't that everyone right
now who is partnered and in conversation? And hasn't
everyone who was trying to have a successful relationship
during quarantine had that conversation?

Well, one day during quarantine, I had dropped my
car off at Beamon Toyota here in Nashville to address the
recall of certain software. After it was serviced, as Erin
drove us to Beamon, I commented that back in Cuba, Alba
mentioned that I might look into the ways in which people
with autism negotiated life.

What I didn't know was Erin had been thinking along
these same lines as we sought to figure out how I could be
more attuned in our relationship. On the drive, I told Erin
that after my brain surgery, I had some sort of neurological therapy and had to put together puzzles to test and
assess my neurological capacity. I was very good at special
puzzles, I told her. I also talked about how in high school,
I was in gifted and talented classes, but because I missed
the required calculus class credits, I couldn't graduate with

honors and so instead took easy classes—band, government, and civics.

As we drove, I talked about going to college, where I always suffered in classes that didn't create conditions for me to imagine and process. I took the same college biology class three times before I passed—I think the professor finally showed compassion for me. I'll never know. Later, though, in my PhD program, I read and loved quantum theory. It wasn't that I couldn't understand the sciences, I said to Erin, it's just that I have to have access to the sciences in a particular way.

My college grades weren't amazing; I really suffered. But once I got into Garrett-Evangelical Theological Seminary in Chicago and began reading what I wanted to read and exploring the philosophical and theological traditions, I found I excelled. Afterward, I went on to earn a PhD in constructive philosophical theology and philosophical ethics; I love theory and philosophy and the ways that these disciplines shape our social realm and practices, but in all that time, it never occurred to me that my brain worked differently. In fact, the academy praised me for my intellectual ability, and I gained even more praise as someone working in these disciplines in new ways, because I was gender nonconforming and masculine presenting. Looking back, I wonder now how many people I've harmed through the years of my education because of my aloofness or inability to read social situations.

Erin listened as I continued talking into new understandings. Being in quarantine and not traveling beyond local roads, I finally had the time to explore these questions that were bubbling up again, now in a very real situation with my current partner.

As we drove, I reached out to a dear friend, Mike McHargue, also known as Science Mike, and asked if he could help me figure out if I was on the autism spectrum by sharing with me his process. He responded graciously and quickly and sent me links to access some assessment tools, which I did as we drove. Each test registered that I was on the spectrum. I found myself surprised and shocked. I wondered and still wonder, Could this be true of me and my brain?

Erin left me off at Beamon, and I got the car but then soon pulled over and googled "adults on the autism spectrum" because I wanted to see if the symptoms they listed resonated with me. They did. I quickly texted Erin the list of symptoms, maybe twenty of them. And close to all of them resonated with me. As I sat in my car, I wondered if I was truly on the autism spectrum, as it seemed, and if Erin would still want to partner with me—would this be too much for Erin? I was scared on several levels to learn this new thing, to wonder what it would mean for me and for Erin, and I was daunted about moving in the world as a public theologian with a diagnosis like this.

After I took the tests and self-assessments Mike shared with me, I texted another dear friend, Hillary McBride, based in Canada. I asked her if she knew anyone who could help me further. I had talked with Hillary previously about my challenges to connect with my body and about my

writing on embodiment and democracy. She was not surprised to hear that I might be on the autism spectrum. Neither was Mike. In fact, Mike thought I was neurodivergent,
he wrote, because he tends to relate better with people who
are neurodivergent. Both Hillary and Mike offered so much
compassion to me as I was figuring this piece out about
myself and how that related to Erin, to my work, to others.

Hillary gave me the name of someone in the greater Nashville area who could facilitate an assessment: Dr. Michelle
McAtee. I reached out to Dr. McAtee and expressed my
desire to learn whether I was on the autism spectrum. After
several clinically framed assessments and a very long session with Dr. McAtee, she confirmed what I was holding,
my body and mind; I was indeed on the autism spectrum.

As we also talked about how Transgender people are
six times more likely to be on the autism spectrum due
to gender and body dysphoria, I found myself surprised to
become more and more settled in my body, something I
had been trying to do through research, writing, reading,
and therapy, but all of that failed to click for me. My brain
isn't normative, and I was trying to do this work in a neuronormative way. I realized that my socialization in the
church and academy had been through neuronormative
people who didn't understand my body or my mind and
had curated such a disconnection from my body!

In that moment, I found myself piecing myself back
together with a new label: *autism*.

First came relief—a relief for me and my partner knowing that those on the autism spectrum were not attuned

to the things around us, that my brain and my body work differently!

It's why I understand myself as NonBinary.

It's why I live in the gray area of life so much.

It's what allows me to have the social courage to say the things that everyone is thinking but no one will say aloud.

Autism is what makes me me in so many ways, and it's what has given me the freedom to think more critically and creatively about my body, my being, my motion in the world.

Yet each of us has some disconnection. Culturally, we are disconnected from everything around us, including our habitat. When we think about our own bodies, we often think of the head as distinctly separate from what we simply call the "body."

At the same time, it is also true that *everything* around us is a body, an idea that's important to unpack. When I was researching for my dissertation, I discovered that philosophy, Indigenous beliefs, rituals, and experiences claim that everything is a body. And while I would cheerfully exclaim yes to this kind of thinking, I continue to limit the scope of this question—*What is a body?*—to the human body, because the human body is what composes our democracy. Now, I know that ecological concerns, climate change, and so many other entities constitute folds of our democracy, and we don't assign agency to nonhuman life, like plants and animals—those lives who are not voting at this present moment in time. So when I am asking this question and ruminating about what is a body, my focus is on living human flesh, the human body and sociosensory material that make up our being in the world.

Culturally, we have left the body by the wayside. And in the aftermath of the murders of George Floyd, Breonna Taylor, Ahmaud Arbery, and countless others, many of us continue to ask, Have we come any closer to understanding what a body is? Have any of us come any closer to respecting what a body is?

During the weeks and years after that conversation with Dr. Antonio and while I was researching the body, I read up on various philosophies on what makes a body.

If René Descartes said "I think; therefore, I am," then what makes a body?

If we know what makes the mind (I think; therefore, I am), what makes the body? And what is a body?

I don't mean to be esoteric here. What makes the body and what is a body are related and important. We are made bodies by proximity and relationship with other bodies— this is a relational process. Singular bodies connected with other bodies make up a larger collection of bodies, which makes up a cultural body. So the idea of relationship seems to be central to becoming a body.

Another thing that makes up a body is mobility. One of the major characteristics of bodies is that they move— across borders, across seas, in relation to others, and more. Bodies are mobile. So what makes up bodies is not only relationships but also the reality of mobility.

Mobility is not about ableism. Every body that is in relation or connection with another is in a dynamic of motion to some degree. All living bodies move in some capacity, not just physically, but emotionally, sensorially in different types of motion. So motion and mobility are part of the dynamic of bodies. When I think about bodies in this way, when I link together mobility and relationship, I come to a clearer understanding that bodies are predicated on connection—the connection of being mobile in a global world and the connection of being able to relate with other bodies across assumed differences. A body must be relational and cannot be reduced to just a mechanism in this world. What has caused so much psychic pain for me is that I was unable to access this piece of connection in my own material body, as it was presented to me in a neuronormative way.

When I think of my own body, one that is born of Mexican flesh and white flesh—a *mestizaje* being—I think about the already existing relationship of ethnicity and culture that exists in my blood, moving through a body in motion, coursing through my veins. When I express myself as a NonBinary Transgender Latinx, I am already in relationship with culture and the cultural body. I wake each morning as a Latinx body, one that has both Indigenous blood and the blood of settler colonialism. I am, as Gloria Anzaldúa wrote, the new *mestizaje* body.

My body is a borderland, a paradox of being and becoming. But for most of my life, I have been disconnected from my body and have only lived from my shoulders to my head. So my pursuit of coming to an understanding of what a body is requires me to analyze my own history of when that separation happened for me and how that separation has been accelerated by my deep socialization in both church and academy. Was it the abuse that I suffered when I was a child? Was it when Mexican men took advantage of me on my grandparents' farm and sexually abused me for years? Was it the faith tradition that created conditions for me to leave an abusive parent? Whatever it was, my coming to my body as an adult, albeit Transgender and Queer, has also been a journey of rediscovering my body in the midst of having a history of being radically disconnected from the flesh that I now know as a body that is becoming bodied with a brain that is neurodivergent.

This is a book about bodies, becoming, and embodiment. I want to talk about human bodies, their scope, the relationship of bodies to themselves, and the relationship of bodies to other bodies so that we can talk about healing our democratic body, our democracy. So in defining what a body is, I am broadening the definition that we have inherited. Bodies are our entire being, and they are in constant motion.

The mobility of bodies is important to discuss because movement—both the internal movement and the external movement—is central to the work of embodiment. These are all a part of the process of becoming embodied—or as I prefer to word it, "becoming bodied"—a way in which to talk about the evolution of embodiment.

The role of becoming is important to name when asking the question *What is a body?* As I formulated in my dissertation project, all bodies are becoming; there is constant change and shifts that are happening that create conditions for bodies to become. And becoming is central to the work of becoming bodied because the more comfortable we are with our own felt sense of the body, the greater the work will be when we intentionally move externally in relation to other bodies and participate in a collective becoming.

I can't help but remember my journey in discovering my own body and each question on that journey:

Am I more than the parts of my body?
Is my body a being in space and time?
What is my capacity as a body?
Can I become bodied in myself and work to become
    bodied within human sociality?

These curiosities embody the work of coming into relationality with what a body is for this project.

Discerning what bodies are and how they fit within the larger landscape of the world is also part of this project. And telling stories that connect the dots between being and becoming can help illustrate the work of becoming bodied.

The word *embodiment* can carry a sort of clinical and sterile texture when it remains trapped in only the theoretical, but embodiment is about connecting with our own flesh, about becoming so very familiar with our bodies that we feel and understand that relationship. That's our beginning place, and it leads us into collective work, as becoming bodied is also the work of healing and reshaping our democracy. This work is part of a collective landscape of using our becoming bodied-ness to relate with others and encourage further the becoming bodied-ness in each of us, one another, our relationships.

Given the complexities of relationships and our own coming into ourselves, we can learn both that our bodies are safe to inhabit and that they are dangerous within and through our most formative primary relationships. We learn danger from our bodies, sense the danger in inhabiting bodies of difference. Often we learn some combination of this: our bodies are safe; our bodies are in danger or dangerous. When we address the existing traumas that keep us from being rooted in our bodies, we get a little closer to the revolutionary work of embodiment and becoming bodied. As I write this in an increasingly digital world and during an accelerated global pandemic, I am aware that these can make for more disconnection from our bodies and from one another than we like. We are glued to our devices and thinking from the shoulders up. Many of us are fully living into the Cartesian split—thinking, being separated—but my hope is that this book will help us learn to drop into our bodies and truly live from a bodied place.

In many respects, my relationship with my body is still on the cusp of becoming. It's an interesting place to be when I've spent years researching the body. My dissertation project was on the body, I tell folks all the time, but not once did the dissertation explore body as a relationship or a relational being. I wrote about the body as something that is becoming yet not as the central organizing feature of what could reshape our democracy. As I intentionally work to unhinge from the self-perpetuating elitism of the academy of higher education, I am more in tune with the ways that the collective body is in pain and is being traumatized and retraumatized. And if the collective body is in this traumatized place, then the individual body, my own body, is also in pain and also holds unprocessed trauma from culture, from what I've inherited, from how I've been socialized, from the *mestizo* blood in my changing body, and much more. We have to remember that oppression is unprocessed trauma on a collective scale, which is what makes the work of embodiment so important if we are going to reshape our cultural—our collective—body.

We experience pain in a variety of ways. It can be a chronic condition; it can be psychic, emotional, or spiritual pain; it can also be cultural pain, pain passed down from the state. This pain affects how we are in relationship with our bodies.

Recently, I was diagnosed with a condition that causes intermittent and chronic pain. At times I am in so much pain that I can barely move or function, and all I can do is breathe and lie down in bed. Sometimes I'm in bed for hours at a time; other times, I'm awakened in the middle of the night with excruciating pain and have to ask for help. During these vulnerable moments, my partner graciously wakes up and gets ibuprofen for me and then begins a process of putting CBD creams on the places that hurt. I try to be in relationship with the pain because I know the pain is part of my lived experience and part of what it means for me to be in this particular body. Yet I observe how pain sometimes can keep people from being in relationship with their bodies, disconnected and far from being able to participate in a becoming relationship with what it might mean to become bodied.

It's important to talk about pain relative to becoming bodied because pain is a universal experience. We all relate to pain differently. And none of us are immune to it. I am trying to chart a relationship with pain so that my process of embodiment is grounded in a lived experience that includes a vast array of experiences, including pain. I am trying to metabolize the pain in my body so that I can become more fully bodied.

When we are able to address the sources of pain, we get a little closer to understanding the impact of such pain and can begin healing processes on both individual and collective scales. This is not easy work and requires many of us to divest from the ways we are conscripted into narratives about pain. The persistence of dominant cultural narratives around hyperindividualism not only has created a disconnect from other bodies but has brought so much undue harm to our understandings. Resmaa Menakem writes about "bodies of culture" as recipients of disproportionate pain. As a result, our collective human body is struggling to heal the social body and doing a poor job because of the ways our bodies continue to hold manifold traumas, including dominant white bodies. This is a complicated and complex terrain we are encountering.

As a result of the global pandemic we find ourselves in as I write this, our world is collectively suffering. The global pandemic has also accelerated economic disparities and anti-Blackness, which furthers the world's collective pain. The question I ask for my body, for our collective bodies, is, How can we work to root ourselves in the evolving relationship of embodiment to create conditions for a new collective body to emerge from the ashes that will inevitably appear?

An important element in talking about the body is understanding the suffering caused by a supremacist culture that insists that our bodies should be machines, should be politically controlled by a dominant culture, a culture that perpetuates a production mentality. The toxicity of capitalism is one we carry in our bodies and our collective body. Even the ways in which time is valued relative to bodies has asphyxiated our bodies into a condition that prevents them from flourishing.

A culture that expects bodies to participate in the transactional time and exchange of capitalism prevents those same bodies from their full expression of movement and expansion. Capitalism forces a limited body, from the shoulders up. And I have not only participated in that kind of body but been deeply conscripted into a life that privileges the head. Every day I work to dismantle this kind of lived experience, and this book charts my limited understanding of embodied living through my own struggle to get into my body, even as the stories shaping me are those of a body engaged in the borderland work of church, academy, and movements for justice.

Capitalism is racialized and benefits the dominant culture with the most access to capital. The ways bodies are dislodged from a connection with the earth through a dominant culture build into a kind of working environment of accelerated production and productivity.

In the early days of the pandemic, many of us were quarantined at home and isolated from our friends, families, and communities, and we were expected to produce on an impossible scale. During this time, I was recording more lectures and sermons and getting paid less. I have always lived the life of the hustle as a theologian pursuing my vocational life in the public square, but the pandemic put things related to embodiment and systems that don't support embodiment into stark relief for me as I struggled to juggle all the balls alongside being on government assistance for unemployment. A lot of my work and labor go unpaid. I am expected to flex my brain and provide analyses and offer presence, all of which go either unpaid or severely underpaid. Capitalism and the folds of the harm of capitalism have accelerated this reality for me and so many others. It's frightening to think about the ways in which our economic system actually accelerates disconnection from body and the earth, from which our body has emerged. No wonder we have created such harmful policies in our communities:

we are disconnected from the earth and the ground of our being.

The relationship between self and other can reshape democracy. We have been taught not to be in relationship with ourselves, and that orientation further accelerates an attitude and practice of not being in relationship with one another. We often live in a suffering we don't even know how to name, failing to learn such basics of embodiment as taking the time to discern our feelings and then letting our feelings be wisdom for an embodied response.

The harmful policies and mechanistic cultural approach have limited our ability to be in relationship with others and develop the kind of relationality that can reshape our culture, which can then curate the necessary change we need in government and policy making, affecting our collective body. We have been stuck being machines for the Man; we have gotten stuck in the transactions of daily life that circumvent our feelings and discard them as something that should remain foreign to us—all instead of having cultural permission to see our feelings and our felt sense of our living bodies as wisdom for these moments. This is particularly true for the culture of whiteness and even shows up in cultures of color in things like respectability politics and in other ways.

It's through ways of stewarding practices grounded in embodied awareness that we can come to have an embodied awareness of things like difference and become a truly antiracist culture. Learning those pathways of embodiment allows us to speak from our bodies and not just rattle off statistics and information that fail to ground an embodied awareness of what is impacting us: our culture. We can move from having talking points to actually having an embodied awareness!

As a conditionally white Latinx (due to my skin color), I am aware of the ways I've been conscripted into whiteness and have assimilated into supremacy culture not only for survival but for achievement as I participate in the meritocracy of higher education. I think about the ways my Mexican mother socialized me into whiteness so that I could have a fighting chance, how attending Catholic school offered me a chance at an education that was informed by and infused with a moral framework that didn't create conditions for me to be an embodied child, and how I pursued higher education and developed a curiosity within academia. Each of these elements not only socialized me into a kind of cultural body (of whiteness) but also stunted my own ability to create an intimacy with my own body. Add to that the complexity of having a brain that is neurodivergent and autistic, a body that is Trans and Queer, creating a lot of confusion for trying to navigate a cultural body of dominance that has no room for someone like me.

I have spent a lot of time thinking about the ways we name and label ourselves—labels like *liberal* and *conservative*, *traditional* and *progressive*—and the ways that those labels and categories don't really capture my theological or political commitments and certainly don't allow for the role of affect and emotion that may help steward practices of embodiment on a personal, interpersonal, and cultural level.

We've got ourselves into a real mess with these categories. They have so polarized us in our thinking that we don't actually know how to be in conversation with the differences we encounter in society and how to imagine a common life with one another. Missing from the culture of the United States are the interlocking realities of transparency, intimacy, and vulnerability. If we could access these within ourselves and with one another, we might be a different cultural body. And if we were a different cultural body, we might be able to imagine another possible world, a robust pluralistic democracy. Are we willing to risk with one another, though, to lean into the felt sense of our bodies to reshape our cultural body?

When I ask these questions about labels and categories, I am thinking through the logic of liberation. While I am conscripted into progressive Christianity, these categories and labels don't reflect my theological and political commitments; they also don't steward a vision for liberation. Part of what we need is to imagine a logic of liberation of self, other, and culture so that we can embody the kind of democracy we long to inhabit. Emancipatory politics is part of how we think through things like embodiment. Coming to understand myself as Trans and NonBinary has helped create conditions for that kind of emancipatory political vision. In the logic of liberation, I only understand this as something done in community, not in isolation, even as this neoliberal society in which we are living creates isolation and accelerates hyperindividualism.

Growing up, I spent my summers in Monterrey, Mexico, with family. Now I am struck by how free they were with emotion and how familiar intimacy was to them. I looked to them with an eagerness to experience this kind of bodily freedom, but my own body was conscripted into a culture that was and has been dominated by white-bodied supremacy. I recall as a teenager holding hands with my Mexican family and feeling a sense of closeness with them and then returning to the United States, where those practices were not available to me. White bodies also suffer from this kind of socialization. Our culture gets made by and through practices of disconnection. Many bodies of culture and color have internalized supremacy culture and are also stunted from being fully embodied, though not all. As I work to define what a body is, I also have to overlay the ways in which the social construct of race and whiteness dominates each of our bodies and turns our bodies into transactions and machines that do not feel yet are emotionally fragile and are suffocating in these moments of deep societal unrest. From Shakespeare and Robert Frost, from Buddhist thinkers and other contemplatives, we have learned "the only way out is through."

We can steward a new body politic that can reshape our democracy by cultivating an embodied awareness of ourselves.

I recently went to Center Hill Lake with my partner for some downtime—to rest, renew, and reimagine. We had access to a boat for half of the first day we were there, so we had a lazy morning, drank our cold brews, and headed to the marina soon after the noon hour. I managed to get the boat out of its slip just fine, and we headed onto our adventure. I've not driven a boat in years, so we were both very curious if I could pull this off! We found a quiet spot to float and swim. I jumped into the water off the front of the boat, making certain that my phone and wallet were not in my pockets and the boat was safely turned off. There, in the midst of a lake that was both warm and cool in layers, I felt my body floating. I thought to myself, *Maybe this is what a body is: a floating, enfleshed reality buoyed by another body* (in this case water). I felt at one with my body and felt so alive in the water. It felt good to be floating. It felt amazing to feel so alive. I'm aware that feeling alive is not guaranteed and is partly tied to my mood and the fact that I was there in the lake with my partner, a person with whom I share a secure attachment. In that moment, with all its connections, I considered the role of attachment theory as profoundly related to coming to terms with what a body is.

We live in a society where attachments are pervasive, but not every attachment is secure. Recently, I learned from a psychotherapist friend of mine, Hillary L. McBride, that nearly 50 percent of all children have secure attachments; the other 50 percent have either insecure or anxious attachments or maybe a combination of the two, and some quite possibly might have an avoidant attachment style. How might these attachments inform our own understanding and relationship with our bodies? For me, my own life has been informed by insecure attachments with my parents, and I wonder how this shapes how I am in relationship with my body or how disembodied I have become.

As I was floating in the water, held by that fierce peace of divinity, I felt one with my body—as though I had a body. I felt embodied. In remembering that sense of unity, that attachment with ourselves and with one another, we can engage practices to reshape our world through loving attachments, attachments that create conditions for an embodied life.

As I try to make the connection between bodies, embodiment, and a vision for emancipatory politics that can reshape our democracy, I discover that attachment theory is helpful. Our culture has an insecure attachment—and probably an anxious attachment too—with itself, and in some cases, there are avoidant attachments within our cultural body. When we can come to terms with our attachment style both as an individual and as a culture, we can begin to imagine our individual selves and our cultural body as an expression that creates conditions for a robust pluralistic democracy. This attachment style is able to hold the multiplicities of differences that live within us as individuals and within our society—our cultural body.

WHOSE BODIES COUNT?

I was taught that I wasn't better than anyone and that no one was better than me. Yet as I was growing up, I also wondered why my skin was a different color than my birth mother's skin. This started when I was maybe five years old. My mother asked me if anyone ever made fun of me for the color of my skin. That's the first time I noticed we were different.

From that moment on, I wondered why people were treated differently, and somehow, in my body wisdom, I knew that not every body counted the same as others, but it would take me years to have both an embodied awareness of this wisdom and the analysis to support this embodied awareness. *Poco a poco*, I say.

As an adult who has lived through the Ferguson uprising, the Black Lives Matter movement (ongoing), and the Charlottesville white supremacist rally, among other protests and uprisings, I worry about the role of power and control and the ways that structural power keeps some bodies down, on the underside of history. I worry about immigrants and refugees and the policies that the government has or doesn't have in place to protect these vulnerable populations. Their bodies count too, don't they?

We live in a society that would have us believe that only certain bodies count, which is why the hashtag #BlackLivesMatter is so necessary. We've created a hierarchy where power over certain bodies has determined their fatal fate. Why is it we don't want everyone to flourish? And why don't we consider the bodies that don't look like us as fully human? I still can't believe that while white women got the vote one hundred years ago, Black women didn't get it until the '60s. Whose bodies count?

Having lived in a time of a persisting global pandemic where the United States continues to have upticks and an enormous case load, I've seen the health disparities revealed in new and staggering ways. Why have Black and Latinx people been at higher risk of Covid-19? Why has the coronavirus seemed to more aggressively attack these communities? Whose bodies really count right now?

Not only did the global pandemic demand answers to this question, but as I watched the murder of George Floyd on various media platforms, I could feel in my bones the answer: not every body counts. This knowledge keeps repeating itself through every twenty-four-hour news cycle and every social media feed. How many other non-Black persons could feel the awfulness of George Floyd's murder? And why does it take violence to assist us in connecting with our bodies?

Not every body counts, I remembered thinking, watching social media videos of him dying. I've known this for years—when Trayvon Martin was murdered, I knew that our country was consuming Black grief but refusing to come to terms with the racial inequity and iniquity that this country harbors. When Mike Brown was shot and killed, his body left lying in a pool of blood in the summer heat, I knew once more that not all bodies count. As a NonBinary Transgender Latinx, I watch the count of Trans murders grow every year; it's a staggering count, many of whom are Trans women of color murdered at the hands of toxic white masculinity.

Not every body counts. No wonder our democracy is a consuming, raging fire around us. Prior to Covid, when I was traveling all the time and chasing airplanes to give talks and live a life as a public scholar and intellectual activist, I was very aware that I could end up in a dumpster somewhere due to being a Transgender person. It might be unlikely because of my skin color, but I knew that because of my gender identity, I might be subject to violence. So when I ask the question *Whose bodies count?* I am also asking if my body counts as we rethink our body politics and our curiosities around how to create conditions for the kind of world we all long to inhabit. "Para todos todo, para nosotros nada," as the Zapatistas say—for everyone everything, for us nothing. I am inspired for another possible world!

I know that I'm not the only one asking these questions—people on all sides of the political spectrum are as well. To myself and to others, I ask if we can steward a politics of being *en conjunto*—and really invest in a world where togetherness can create a politics of what is possible for each of us, all of us. The term *en conjunto* is not easily translated into English. The best translation is "together" or "being together," but it is a richer, more robust phrase suggesting something beyond just togetherness. It's like a ride-or-die partner! Can we have that kind of political orientation in our world today?

When we do the work of unmasking whose bodies count and build the *en conjunto* relationships, we can begin to repair what's broken. And I want to start with my own body and the ways my body has counted and not counted. My story and the stories that have shaped me point me toward a better body politic that can create conditions for an embodied life. My story and my body awareness begin with knowing I am an imperfect being who is—each day—becoming. As my story adds to other stories, I trust they will point us toward the imaginative possibilities that the beloved embodied community can be and become. Another possible world, if you will.

I don't know why my dad married my mother; I don't know if he thought about the racial implications of himself as a white American marrying my birth mother, a Mexican immigrant. But I know this: my mother did. Marrying was her way out of dysfunction and poverty, though as with the things we all hope to leave but still carry, I have seen how dysfunction and poverty have followed her.

In the mid-'70s, when I was born, the world was a different place than it is now—or at least that is what I was taught. My paternal grandparents showered me with love—a love I experienced, an embodied love. They were amazing, these white-bodied folks. My grandfather was a white man from Texas who dropped out of law school to marry my grandmother and farm on her family's land; my grandmother was a demure West Texas woman and a school nurse. I developed a secure attachment with them. They held me with a fierce sense of love.

I never remember my father being at home; I think he left soon after I was born, and my parents divorced when I was five or six. There are pictures of him holding me with a smile on his face, but his presence wasn't in the home. Until I was twelve years old, I lived with a single parent. And in those twelve years, I learned hard and difficult things, among them that my body wasn't important. While I loved my grandparents, I didn't live with them, and learning how to be in this world at an early age without secure immediate attachments to caregivers and without appropriate emotional support likely caused me to disconnect from my body. I moved up into my head, where I was able to imagine a different and more secure life. This life included resources and safety: plenty of food, electricity running all the time—and no violence. In these formative years, I likely internalized the poverty, violence, and intermittent light through my wish for a different life. And while I held on to the hope for a different life, among the other things I probably internalized was learning that my body didn't count.

At that time, we mostly had our basic needs met, since my birth mother worked for Sears, Roebuck and Co. and my grandparents helped us out a lot, making sure I always had access to my Catholic school uniforms (even if they were from a secondhand shop). Despite this, my body felt the lack and the loss. I've internalized that. And on top of that, I experienced physical and emotional abuse from my birth mother. She didn't know how to handle her anger then; she still doesn't. As a young child, I didn't know how to create boundaries. Now in my adult life, that is the work that I continue to do with my biological family: I create boundaries, and I go to therapy every week to stay sane in a world that discounts people who look like my birth mother.

She worked constantly, almost every day of the week. I learned to occupy myself. I learned how to play by myself, climb trees, and ride motorcycles with the neighborhood boys. I learned how to be alone—and I learned how to live in my head because it was safer. I learned how to have relationships that were cerebral rather than embodied because it was safer.

Trauma is a fucking nightmare when you're a kid. I live with the scars to this day.

At an early age, I learned anger. Not the kind of righteous anger that is needed to change systems and rebuild this democracy. What I mean is I learned about anger, how to be afraid of anger, as violence against me stunted my ability to be in my body and have a right relationship with my body. To this day, I am still scared of anger. It's amazing to me how the body remembers and how that memory reverberates out, sometimes reverberating out harm when harm has been internalized. The body remembers their birth mother—I have a lot of compassion for mine, even as I am unable to come close to her emotionally. In fact, I don't even know the woman who gave birth to me. Yet my body remembers the harm and the ways my birth mother's violence perpetuated my own body's disembodied survival response.

Violence permeates our communities, especially communities of culture. Many of us have latched on to violence as a way to leverage power to get our needs met. And here, both trauma and attachments come into play. I consider the trauma my birth mother endured and the ways that those kinds of attachments got buried in her psyche, which then motivated her to act in a certain way. Collectively, we are living through traumatic times, and many of us have been living through traumatic times our entire lives. Some of us are only just coming into the awareness of the trauma and the complexities of that trauma.

The members of my biological family were witnesses to trauma and violence. My birth mother inherited this trauma as an attachment, and this attachment formed in her the wounds and scars that played out in all her relationships. Again, oppression is unprocessed trauma on a collective scale.

Isn't this the reality of our culture and society? Isn't this the reality of our democracy?

This is the road I've taken in the work I've done. I left my birth mother at age twelve, moving in with my white father in the Hill Country of San Antonio, Texas. The electricity was always on, and affluence and privilege and power were in abundance. Realizing I couldn't embody the kind of power my father expected me to embody, I left him and went to college in West Texas. To become my own person. I started therapy and came out as Queer and then Transgender.

I've done a lot of leaving and coming into myself.

But not all the coming into myself resulted in an embodied life. I carry with me the trauma of not only my mother's violence but other violence, of being sexually abused on my grandparents' farm for many years. Even as I did a lot of leaving, I kept that secret from everyone. I didn't know how to talk about how the Mexican workers on my grandparents' farm lured me into their house and touched me in ways that I shouldn't have been touched and showed me things a child never should have seen or learned. Keeping that secret, I continued to internalize that shame. Only when I was safe in relationship, attached, secured was I able to come out about the abuse. My body didn't count then—that was the message I received. So why does it count now, I wonder?

Discounting the body is prevalent in families, cultures, governments, and politics. Even Christian theology discounts the body. The body was written out of the faith and then further demonized by Greek thought. Early Christian thinkers picked up from there, shaping Christian tradition. So no wonder we don't know how to have a relationship with our bodies. No wonder we don't have a body politic that nurtures a healthy democracy, offering emancipatory policies.

I think back to my summers visiting family in Mexico, remembering how my body moved to the cultural rhythms of that time. I remember seeing how people treated one another. I also remember coming back home to the States and not seeing the same kind of respect given in interpersonal relationships. I internalized this bad behavior, probably enacting the same bad behavior that society modeled to me. That kind of behavior has its talons in me.

In Mexico, being around bodies of culture, I feel different. I feel alive. I feel seen. I feel the different contours of relationship. But as a body politic, as a society, I don't experience this kind of generative relationality. Why is that? Because we don't believe that all bodies count.

I saw that when my white father worked with people; he would use power and manipulative tactics to get what he wanted. At whatever cost. He was horribly racist and bigoted. When these kinds of relationships are modeled to us, we not only mimic that behavior when we socialize with people; we internalize it in ourselves as we encourage those around us to internalize what they see.

As a young person who attended church and learned a different way to be, I questioned the way my white father treated people. But when I saw the heteropatriarchy in the church, how women were marginalized and minoritized bodies were treated, I wondered how different the church really was from my very secular white father.

Even our faith communities exhibit bad body politics that don't count all bodies as valuable. Especially white faith communities. It was only when I moved to Chicago for seminary that I saw a broader swath of *en conjunto* relationships and cultural practices and was introduced to a variety of understandings and theoretical models of the histories of bodies, relationship, and politics—beginning to give me a handle on the very bad behavior of our society—as well as potential models that offered hope beyond "violence begetting violence."

Living in Texas, I was used to seeing bodies like mine and understood *Mexican American* and *Latinx* from a Texas perspective. When I moved to Chicago, I learned that the term *Latinx* was very broad and that there were so many other bodies in the greater Chicagoland area that had been socialized Latinx in such different ways than my Texan upbringing.

I still have kept that Texas pride of being from a state that values hospitality and deep postures of welcome, but I wrestle with the history of rampant racism of my birth state even as I glean from observing the ways that bodies of culture can actually transform our society. Investing in a body politic that values all bodies, we come a little closer to reshaping our realities. It's work that takes practice. I've learned firsthand through watching Chicago politics that not all bodies matter, what anti-Black racism is, and how Black America is being systematically executed by politics and policies and white governance.

As I've moved on to other parts of the United States, I've seen how not all bodies matter. When I was living in Denver, Colorado, for my PhD program, I saw immigrants treated with the general texture of antagonism toward those seeking a safe and better life from their war-torn countries. When we begin to unmask these realities and trace their origins, we see those ancient anti-body Christian teachings and settler-colonial powers at play in our society.

We normalize answers to what bodies count, and not only do we enact manifold violence against those who don't count, we also culturally and societally seek to disenfranchise bodies of culture because they don't count.

Good is a contested term. What makes a good society? What makes a good body? We've normalized whiteness and the white body and so count that as good and true. Perhaps we would even call whiteness beautiful. But if we look at what we call "good" as reserved for a particular kind of body, we see that not every body is good. Because not every body counts.

Flipping the script on that narrative starts with who we are in relationship with and how we understand our own body in relationship with bodies of culture. The new script asks what kinds of attachments we have to our own bodies and the bodies around us. It is a script of a body politic that weaves together the tapestry of difference that defines America on new terms. Part of saving our democracy is learning to live an embodied life, because when we learn to integrate head with heart with body, a new and generative relationality with our own bodies emerges. This is a relationality of interpersonal connections that have the opportunity to impact our cultural body.

We might ask what bodies count, but the questions that necessarily follow it come with challenges: Do we have an imagination for that kind of democratic body, that kind of interpersonally connected society? Do we *want* that kind of change? And what might it require of us? Giving up long-held beliefs that are actually harming us and our society? Getting out of our heads and stewarding a more heart-forward connection—a real connection—with our bodies and the bodies around us? Can we shift what we've considered "good" right now out of a contested frame and into a garden of melodic becomings that takes the politics of radical difference as the stepping-stone to reshaping whose bodies count?

Politics is a term used to indicate how we organize our thoughts and behaviors. Of course, we've colloquially been using this term to refer to Democratic and Republican policies. But politics is really an organizing principle around ways we shape and shift our society. When I think about the politics of radical difference being the stepping-stone to reshaping our bodies and our body politic, I'm referring to the ways that difference can be the meter. Difference is that thing without a norm—it's an effort to destabilize norms and allow for multiplicity. The politics of radical difference is a fold of multiplicity in our behaviors and thoughts.

* * *

The difficult start we're called to make is with all the privileges many of us have. For instance, my body counts in a lot of places because I have three little letters after my name: PhD. I am legitimated in ways other people are not. I bring this up not to discount the hard work I've done to achieve my education but to talk about how my assimilation into systems of higher education was not only a survival skill but a narrative I internalized from the time I was a kid. My birth mother told me when I was young that education was my way out. So at an early age, I learned to apply myself from my cerebral place, living my life from the shoulders up. My work now is to relax into my body and figure out how to create the kind of world we all long for. So I am counted as "good" because I've achieved education, but I am not counted as "good" because I am Transgender and Latinx. It's a mixed bag. And my embodied life is still emerging on a path of liberation for me as I also learn what that looks like on a collective scale.

How do we dismantle a caste system that reserves what is "good" only for those legitimated by the logic of dominance? This is the pernicious evil that creates such a disembodied society. As a culture and society, we have come to value the professionalization of life and work. But what if those who don't have the same path; can we imagine a society and culture that values different paths and composts the existing hierarchies and caste systems? How can we create a culture and society that values all bodies? We are in a moment where unless Black lives matter, we are missing the mark. With this, we must figure out how to make visible Brown bodies, because if we perpetuate the Black/white binary, we end up making people like me and other Brown bodies invisible. *Poco a poco.*

I don't necessarily have the answers or know how to do this kind of work, but what I do have is an imagination of a different future. For those who look to books to understand how to be antiracist, my take is this work is really found in the body, in becoming embodied, and in relationships. We can read all the books, know all the histories of the displacement of Black people, Indigenous folks, and non-Black people of color globally and locally, but unless we have an embodied awareness of this, we won't really be able to overhaul the acceleration of the anti-Blackness and anti-people of color mentality that is so pervasive throughout the world. We must learn how to compost the bullshit.

And let me also add that the growing dualism and binary of Black and white in the race wars renders people like myself and immigrant folks—Brown and Latinx—invisible. We must find a way to cultivate conversations around race that address both the acceleration of anti-Blackness and the growing binary of Black and white so that non-Black persons of color are not rendered invisible by the machinations of a neoliberal race war that seeks to preserve and fortify whiteness. I am reminded here that even the phrase *person of color* reifies whiteness. We must find a different way to speak about difference and embody not only a hermeneutic of suspicion but also a hermeneutic of retrieval.

Among the ways supremacy culture works, especially white-bodied supremacy, is its dependence on binaries. So the division between Black and white is playing into the very system that supremacy culture is engineered to perpetuate. When we move out of these dualistic categories around human bodies, we can imagine narratives around bodies of culture that create conditions for all bodies to count in a way that is aligned with the logic of liberation. Many of us are not well practiced in nondual thinking to hold the reality of *both/and*. This is where someone who is NonBinary Transgender can help facilitate opportunities to shift the public discourse into both/and dimensions.

Deeply invested in the politics of both/and, I believe reshaping our body politic begins when we value all bodies equally and begin to restructure our society and culture along the lines of counting everyone as good, not just the select few who can go to college and make a livable wage, not just those who accumulate wealth. *Good* is not merit based, even though we have engineered good/bad as binary thinking into our society, culture, and policies and engineered good with the meritocracy of this culture.

The notion of good dates back to people like Aristotle and Thomas Aquinas, who theorized good as being directly connected to our character and being a good human, one that is godly, even—and we have forgotten that historical memory. Perhaps that is one of the failures of understanding what bodies count, because we've erected an understanding of what is good as those who are directly connected to power, access, and privilege, which often equals white-bodied folks. We value the all-American dollar over humanity; we value transactions over connections. We value accumulating wealth and things over making sure everyone has their most basic needs met. Is this an attachment to scarcity? I know it took a long time for me to get out of the mindset of what my next meal would be. How do we reshape our body politic to one that leverages abundance instead of accelerating attachments to scarcity politics that ultimately harm all of us? How do we reimagine what is good in light of the acceleration of things like meritocracy in our culture?

I was well into graduate school when I discovered that after I ate a meal, I would start worrying and wondering when my next meal would be available, a response coming from a place of trauma and scarcity. The trauma doesn't necessarily go away, and these wounds are very deep, but in acknowledging both, we learn how to relate with the trauma on terms that allow for us to be healthy and ultimately embodied.

So during the global pandemic, I could have applied for food assistance, but instead, I sat with the resources that I had and learned to lean into abundance while not letting my trauma or unhealed attachments drive this bus. What I had was enough, and learning that lesson during a time of globalized trauma was important for me. I began metabolizing the trauma narratives of scarcity during this time and leaned into an awareness of abundance—into a practice of reminding myself that "I will be OK" and "all shall be well."

When we learn to honor our bodies—and by this I mean all our bodies—a part of that honoring work is healing our untamed trauma and our attachments to it.

The body is conscripted into these trauma narratives that tell us we aren't enough and that we don't have enough. When we are able to unite head, heart, and body and lead from a grounded place in our restoried selves that isn't constantly jerked around by our untamed trauma narratives, we can get really close to what living a life in our bodies looks like. When we tell the truest truths about what bodies count and learn to flip the script on the racism, misogyny, and supremacy cultures that keep the narrative in place that only dominant bodies matter, we move toward a cultural body politic that counts every body—and I mean *every body.*

This requires that we stop fighting the poor and fight to eradicate poverty, creating a better body politic. When we shift white governance toward governance that values American difference, multiplicity, and all that is emerging, we begin to adapt and call forth a different body politic. This does not happen in one election cycle or from a unilateral vote for change. This happens when we repeat the intention until we reach a different body politic. It takes practice, and practice can make a more perfect union. When we get up each day and value every body and live out the principles that allow for Black lives to not only live and matter but flourish, we get a little closer; these moments also fortify the lives of Indigenous people and other non-Black people of color. When we are able to relate from the place of our grounded embodied stories, we reshape ourselves and those with whom we are in relationship, and that's when things will shift toward a new cultural phenomenon that is grounded in embodied wisdom.

But to get there, we first have to reckon with the reality that not every body counts, beginning with imagining a different future. One where existing supremacies are composted into the kind of society we long to see—a society that is foregrounded by love and where embodied wisdom is the first step. When we can practice that kind of society, we get closer to counting every body as good and valuable and not just those who can earn a dollar or accumulate wealth.

This work demands taking our attachment to scarcity and renewing our imagination with abundance. This work demands learning how to live life from an embodied standpoint and not just from talking points. This work demands taking trauma and dysfunction seriously, as when I left my home in Texas to attend college, even as I am still working out the traumas with their talons in me. This personal work is something I understand might take a lifetime for me to undo. And that is OK because I want to leave the world in a better place than how I found it. I want to eradicate violence and poverty and harmful governance in exchange for revolutionary love, kindness, empathy, and compassion. Because when we *suffer with* one another, we come close to the pain that impacts us all. Suffering with one another is not something we do very often. When we go back to the Latin root of *suffer with*, we arrive at the translated word *compassion*. To have compassion is to suffer with. As

Frederick Douglass wrote, "I prayed for twenty years but received no answer until I prayed with my legs." To suffer with is to pray with our body, to get our hands and feet dirty with the suffering of the world. *El mundo late.* The world palpitates for hope and change. When we can be honest about that pain and generate relationships from the place of empathy and compassion, we not only restructure the connection to other bodies; we restructure our bodies, our nervous systems, acquainting them with the kindness of compassion. A different framework emerges for living with one another. When we do this, we gain the capacity to ultimately reshape our democracy to be one where every body counts and not one person is left behind. *Poco a poco nos liberamos.* Little by little, we get free.

The *suffering with* that creates changes in ourselves and the democratic body requires the deep inner work of changing ourselves and divesting from the bullshit that keeps us acting through privilege and trauma in ways that marginalize those counted as other, those who are otherwise beings. When we do this inner work, we begin to see the underside of history with better eyes, eyes that invite relationship. When we turn from the violence of humanity and turn toward relationally centered practices like nonviolent communication, we reduce gaslighting and other forms of diminishment and erasure. To count every body as human and valuable is essential, difficult work, but I believe in the work of community and the ways that being in community can transform society. And I believe in the power of love. I've seen how love, when enacted in revolutionary ways, can hold the complexities of each of our multiplicities and call forth a more perfect union. I believe in our capacity to guide one another into this new vision of humanity. And I believe we can learn to love ourselves enough to love those who we had formerly called other, those who are not like us.

When we restory ourselves through love, compassion, kindness, and empathy—practices that we all need help with—we learn a different anthropology, and this informs the spiritual practices we choose to live into. Each spiritual intuition is an ethical practice, so these things matter! When we turn to innovating this new vision of humanity, we are innovating and animating the process of becoming. When we innovate the process of becoming, we become familiar with change as the only constant and turn toward change and away from the fear we have so long attached ourselves, our bodies, to. When we animate the process of becoming, we lean into the multiple processes of change that becoming initiates.

In leaving the church, earning a PhD, coming to terms with who I am as a NonBinary Transgender Latinx, dosing testosterone each week, deepening my antiracist awareness, and learning about embodiment, I've encountered a lot of change. And becoming is never easy. Becoming is the work of inner and outer mechanisms. Becoming is our invitation for a new humanity. Becoming is the work that creates conditions for answering the question *Whose body counts?*

II

BECOMING

*B*ecoming has a long philosophical history dating back to Lucretius and to the first atomic theory. I would call this history mechanical, brittle even. Becoming is something I think of in terms of sudden and prolonged change, a kind of condition within its nature that further encourages change too that is enfolded into processes of change and a relationship with change. Yet *becoming body* is something I understand as changing and emerging from a relational perspective, a space and place where change happens because of filial connections.

Drawing again from the philosophy work of Gilles Deleuze, the concept of becoming emerges and is explored in the following chapters. And to consider becoming, I'm helped by a concept proliferating for some years now in Queer theory and other theories: assemblage. An assemblage is a collection of any number of things that may appear alike or different in their materiality that are gathered into a single new context or a singularity. Even in its singularity, assemblage always retains its particularity. Take, for example, this book. It is an assemblage, a collection of lines of thoughts and lines of flights, its changes and movements, all collected into a single container called a *book*.

Becoming, in its singularity and particularity, then, is the specificity of change or movement within an assemblage. And becoming is necessarily related to rupture, to change, to movement—in this sense, of something taken from one context and placed in another, with its multiplicities of relationship. When any change or movement within an assemblage occurs, becoming emerges. And when one piece of the assemblage is grafted or drawn into the territory of another piece, the value of the element and birthing a new unity are what emerge. It is as if becoming is a midwife of sorts, allowing for the emergence of a new unity, a new whole, a new becoming.

BECOMING BODY

Becoming is a playful, dynamic term—and it has a complicated and sophisticated history within the field of philosophy. It's important to explore becoming in multiple ways so that we can think more collectively about things requiring becoming, like social change, collective liberation, and a healthy vision of democracy.

Embodiment is in a dynamic relationship to becoming, and both are rooted in the motion that already envelops us all. Motion with ourselves and the cultural body is what is at stake in these moments. When we participate in the multiplicity of motion and movements, we can learn to reorder and reshape our cultural body so that there are healthy attachments to change. This begins with understanding motion and movement as emerging from creative energies found within our bodies.

As with most things in my innermost world, I find concepts tantalizing, even titillating. I fell in love with philosophy in college and continue to return to the *love of wisdom* (which is what *philosophy* means in Greek), trying to connect the dots between what we have inherited in our conceptual frameworks and what gets played out in reality.

I continue to be drawn to a particular rendering of *becoming* formulated by Gilles Deleuze in his philosophical writings because he doesn't reduce becoming to merely mechanistic change, which Georg Wilhelm Friedrich Hegel does. Hegel was considered the philosopher of becoming before Gilles Deleuze came onto the philosophical stage. And many people are influenced by both figures. I have a distinct leaning toward Deleuze and thinkers like Michel Foucault because their work was embodied. Both were very active in the political uprisings in France following the war. While Hegel formulated becoming in terms of mechanistic change, I understand becoming as more of a process of iteration. Most agree that the simplistic and common understanding of becoming is some sort of fundamental change, but that is where the philosophers diverge, as Deleuze and Foucault ask, What if becoming was more complicated than that, especially as it relates to the singular body that is becoming that is in relationship to a collective body that is becoming?

What if? What if these "changes" created conditions for a revolution of values or a change in our body politic? At the time I was writing this book, some months before the 2020 election, I saw becoming all around me. Not only through the political rhetoric but also through the images in my dreams. I had a dream of Joe Biden in khaki shorts and Kamala Harris in dress clothes. Our dreams are a part of our becoming too. Perhaps I needed a more human Biden to show up in my dreams, dressed not in a suit but in clothes recognizable to me as play clothes. Perhaps my relationship with my dream state and becoming informed me that I need more play in my life. Dreams often come as question marks.

When I was in seminary, I was invited to think about play. For years, I hadn't played, not since I was a kid. Play, I thought, was something children do, not what budding serious theologians do. But throughout my years of dreaming and becoming, I started looking differently at play: if we don't have play as part of our social change game plan, we might fall into the traps of understanding becoming on mechanistic terms. It is not the mechanistic—the ladder steps to power—that leads us into the dynamism of change. It is, among other things, play. And with play comes pleasure!

Play, as we know, is a process of letting loose and participating in dynamics that facilitate precisely this component of becoming I am attempting to share. The iteration of play in our dreams and in our waking life is part of how we get into the rhythm of becoming. Play can be lots of things, have many elements, but one thing play does is set things in motion for them to become. When we play, we often experience pleasure too. I wonder how so many of us are bereft of both play and pleasure in our current body politic.

Becoming, as I understand it and perhaps how Gilles Deleuze leads to understanding it, is a phase between two states, or a range of states, that is in motion. Becoming is the relationship between melody and harmony; it is a refrain. When we talk about becoming in terms that aren't mechanistic, we talk about it being "on the way" toward something that does not have a finite end. It is in motion in a way that is similar to our body's chemistry—just think of that amazing image of the interplay of the double helix.

To imagine what is possible with becoming requires using our imagination and digging deep into our conscious (and also) dreaming self. As I think about the journey I am on relative to becoming (em)bodied, I think also about the movement of the larger world, relations that are beyond my tangible reach. I also think about the ways that becoming cannot be divisible—as it is a process of change that involves relationships and connection, a momentum that cannot be broken. The helix chain of becoming is a movement within us on a cellular level and on a macrolevel; we might not be able to see the change, but the change is emerging and emanating from local and nonlocal changes.

Becoming has been used as a buzzword. And I don't want to reduce it to being a mechanistic token helping us "get into our bodies" because I want us to hold the complexity of the process of what it means to become (em)bodied—our relationship with our own body and the collective relationship with our cultural body, the play and pleasure of a becoming democracy.

It's not just about walking or running or working out. Sure, they might enable some part of the process of becoming, but becoming is in relationship with time, memory, and future—where the future is cast as an infinite becoming. We can't exactly say what the future is.

Becoming is also an immanent process. It is that thing that is with us at all moments and is all around us, not transcendent and intangible, though it might feel as though it is out of our tangible reach. Becoming is that thing that produces the kind of systemic and molecular change that we want to see in the world. Becoming mobilizes our being in the world in ways that set us all in motion, the kind of motion that can be seen and felt and not seen and not felt. It is a both/and process of the microscopic and the sensory motion that we might feel on our skin at times. Becoming is complicated and in infinite motion.

Remember what it's like to walk in the hot sun? Beads of sweat bubble up on your skin, you're out of breath, and your pace slips. Those are moments of becoming. That's a becoming at a molecular state. We also know that becoming happens on a macrostate, and when these becomings enter into relationship, as they are always in relationship, our being changes state and function.

Because this book is on the process of becoming (em) bodied, I want to hold the philosophical category of becoming close because it can help us chart this journey of our bodies coming into better relationship with themselves and in better relationship with other bodies. These are the molecular states of change—our being—that are in motion in perpetual ways.

Becoming is an iterative process. There is repetition, like that of a refrain in a musical score. When we harness this iterative process, we come into relationship with becoming. Why is this important for becoming (em)bodied? Because becoming (em)bodied in its iterative process of cellular, molecular, and macrochange hinges on the kind of relationship we have with our being. Becoming is fundamentally about being. However, becoming doesn't stop with the question of being. The question of being accelerates our epistemology, our study and production of knowledge. This then impacts our ethics. Being, thinking, and doing are all imbricated to produce conditions of becoming. Because becoming is actually an accelerating state and in relationship with lived reality and the love of knowledge and wisdom (the discipline of philosophy), our ways of knowing and our ways of acting are accelerated.

These three elements or pillars of life—lived reality, our ways of knowing, and our question of being and becoming—shape the rest of the refrain and the iterative processes. Becoming is not just the Big Bang but all that came before the Big Bang and all that came after the Big Bang and the Big Bang itself, if it's helpful to think about becoming in evolutionary terms. We rarely think about our being from a metaperspective or metaphysical perspective, but these points of view in relation with each other give us some interplay, distance, texture, and nonattachment to our ideas—when being is related to our ways of knowing (and not knowing).

Here's where becoming as a process bears its relationship to being (em)bodied. This relationship between becoming and the body is essential for knowing the felt sense of what is happening. And when we come to an awareness and produce knowledge of the felt sense of what is happening, we are in relationship with becoming. It is both a microscopic interior awareness and a tangible felt awareness or sense. Becoming is both large and small. In fact, becoming is all around us because all things are in motion, expanding and contracting. If this is the case on a metaphysical level, then it also is true on a material and physical level. All things are becoming and in relationship to becoming. As Gloria Anzaldúa says, "*Vale la pena*; do work that matters!"

So if everything is in motion and we can see the acceleration of motion through every aspect of the physical, social, interior worlds—through immigration, through dreams, through the sun on our skin, through technology and the speed at which information processes, and through the ways that even these words are appearing on a computer screen as I type them for this book—then we can also say that becoming (em)bodied is in relationship with this motion.

In the language of theology and pan*en*theism, we might say that God—in motion and relationship—is in all things and willing all things to come to life. In the language and lens of animism, it is the cognization and awareness that all things are endowed with spirit and life, something that Christian theology erased and never incorporated into the life of the church. Whatever our orientation to this microscopic and macroscopic movement, we can call it becoming. We can also see that this movement is in relationship with all other things. So when I think about how becoming (em)bodied can reshape our democracy, it is because I believe that this ongoing movement can shape a cultural body precisely because we are in relationship with the motion, the movement, the spirit, the life of becoming.

Let me remedy some of this headier material with a return to play and pleasure. When I think about becoming, I think about play and the iterative process that is our relationship to play. When we play, we are experiencing all sorts of emotions and movements and pleasure. We embrace the melody and harmony of play and even participate in its refrain: we want more! When we are engaged in this activity of play, we are in relationship with the process of becoming. When we are in the process of becoming, we have a chance not just to imagine a different way to be and become but to have a felt sense of the power of our becoming. Through the process of play, we have this all.

Yesterday, as I was exercising, I was thinking about how to write about my somatic—my (em)bodied journey. I was doing circuit exercises on Zoom because everything is on Zoom these days. I was feeling the beads of sweat bubbling up on my face, arms, and legs. My body was shedding a layer of its toxins and was in process with its relationship with becoming. I was in motion, my cells were doing their thing, and my body was changing on a molecular level; I was participating in becoming without even realizing it. It was happening because of all the pieces set in motion—from my body to technology to my imagination of what I want to become. I want to have a relationship with my body, a healthy attachment to my own being, so that I can participate in the world in a way that will make it a better place.

The plumb line of becoming is this iterative process where you are in the process of becoming—being made into—a better person who can contribute to the healing of our societal and cultural wounds. "*Vale la pena*; do work that matters."

The process of becoming helps facilitate our relational awareness of how we can be as a people. We are so locked into ways of thinking that actually undermine our becoming a healthy and free and cosmopolitan democracy. I'm not suggesting that the uprisings aren't necessary; they absolutely are if we are to get to a different place (remember, everything is in motion, and rupture is a part of the process of becoming), but when we actually harness our becoming (em)bodied process and learn to cocreate with others—with God or the Divine, even—we reshape what is possible in the world. Our ability to be (em)bodied is also in relationship with our capacity to make change. This process of becoming is not just a singular individual thing; it is in relationship with all other things. So to chart a better world, we begin first to chart a better understanding of ourselves and have a felt sense of our bodies so that we can cultivate healthy attachments in the world that then mobilize other bodies, including our cultural body, to become well.

Becoming is—beyond and through and in relationship to this theoretical philosophy—also a story. Ideas take (em)bodied reality forming within my body, which is in motion, which dreams, which sweats, which lives in my story of becoming.

I wake up every day in a body I know and do not know because my body is becoming.

On Sunday mornings, I perform a ritual of that becoming.

While the coffee is brewing in the kitchen, I shuffle into the bathroom half awake and grab off the shelf above the toilet a little blue backpack that my partner got for me for Christmas in 2019. Inside is all my testosterone-related stuff: alcohol wipes, big needles to draw the medicine from its vial, smaller needles to inject the medicine, and a syringe. I sit down on the couch in the living room and, with a larger needle in hand, begin to measure out the appropriate dose of testosterone to inject.

Once I have it, I take an alcohol wipe and gently swab an area two inches away from my belly button. I alternate sides each week so the injection sites aren't overwhelmed. After swabbing my stomach, I attach the larger needle to my syringe and begin the draw. You have to insert air into the medicine so that it will filter into the needle and can then be measured into the syringe. I do that, and with the bottle turned upside down, the testosterone (or *T*, as I call it) begins to fill my syringe.

In 2019, on the fiftieth anniversary of the Stonewall riots, I decided I would start introducing the alternative hormone (T) to my body on a weekly basis. My dose of T is only 0.3—that's half of a regular dose of T—considered a "microdose," but now I inject 0.4, which is not technically a microdose any longer. I fill the syringe with the T and then gently remove the draw needle from the medicine bottle. I switch the needles, attach the smaller needle to my syringe, and I am ready to inject the T into my body. Testosterone is a hormone, but I refer to T as a necessary vitamin for my survivability.

But first, I breathe. I wonder what this dose will do for me. How will my body change? How will my body become? How will the iterative process of dosing T shape and shift my body; the imagined movement and evolution of my becoming body foreshadow liberation in my mind. I am curious; I am in awe; I wonder who I am becoming as a result of these weekly injections.

Every week my body changes, and I notice these changes the most the day before I slow down to take my T shot. Already my voice is deeper, and I notice hair on my chest. I am becoming; my body is becoming. I celebrate this.

My partner places their hand on my knee, as if they were welcoming my becoming into our home, and in this moment of reflective intimacy, I push the plunger on the syringe, and the T enters my body. The testosterone is thick, so it takes some muscle to actually give the shot, and once I manage to get all the hormone into the fat of my belly, I remove the syringe and discard the needles into a large sharps container for after-use syringes. I breathe some more and finally am ready for my cup of cold-brew coffee!

"I am becoming," I exhale. That movement compels me into deeper folds of relating with myself, both true and imagined. Could my becoming self be paving the way for the logic of liberation?

Even as I lean into my T-dosing Sunday ritual, where I imagine what my body might become, I know that my imagination helps me in becoming the embodied person I long to be. I think about the body. And think about the body that I long to have. Not a fatter or skinnier body; I'm talking about the gendered body I have. Assigned and labeled female at birth, I have grown into adulthood believing I am neither male nor female. I transcend the static gender binary.

The body I have is light-skinned and conditionally white, so I move in the world with power, access, and privilege. I am also masculine of center, meaning; I express myself in some form of masculinity. And I am also Trans NonBinary and gender nonconforming. And my mind works within the autism spectrum, where I miss social cues, don't always know how to respond in certain situations, and depend on friends and comrades to help me through sometimes difficult interpersonal situations because my brain doesn't compute in neuronormative ways. In addition to weekly T dosing and leaning into the body I envision for myself, I hope soon to have top surgery, where my chest will be differently contoured and I will fit more easily into my body.

I want to wake up each morning in a body that I know, but even that is up in the air as I imagine what kind of body I long to have.

Each Sunday, as I wake up in a body that I do not know, I am grateful that I can perform my ritual of the insertion of T. This is important to name because too many people wake up in a body they do not know or, worse yet, wake up feeling disconnected from their body. I know I have been disconnected from my body and have been on a five-year journey seeking to re-mem-ber myself and heal the wounds that have caused me to be disconnected from my body. In fact, when I found a therapist after I moved for my faculty job in the Bay Area, the first thing I said to her was "I want to have a relationship with my body!"

To this day, I'm still working on that. I am becoming!

I have spent a lifetime in academia, negotiating the politics of higher education, and I have spent just as much time in the church, negotiating the bad dogma and theology that would otherwise erase me, harm me, and dispose of me as not having anything to offer the communities I've been a part of. I have worked hard to use my gifts of contemplation and thinking to connect with lived experience, but I have not achieved that. Not yet. I am still becoming. As San Salvadoran Jesuit priest Ignacio Ellacuría wrote, "Contemplativo en el camino de la justicia"—contemplative in the way of justice.

When I began thinking about bodies, I first thought of my body—unrecognizable to me and unintelligible to the world. I know my body will shift and change as I continue injecting testosterone; even the slightest amount will change me. This is a good thing; it is important.

Changing me changes the world. We need these changes in the world so that we can survive. I worry, though, about those of us who are Transgender and gender nonconforming. Will we disrupt and defeat the violence, or will the violence intended for us consume us to the point of no return? I don't know. The world is also becoming even as we, ourselves, are becoming.

When I think about our collective body, I wonder if we have an imagination for what bodies should be in this moment. What bodies count in this moment? Which bodies have access in this moment and future moments? I consider how my body has some access, and the more masculine I become, the greater power, access, and privilege I will receive. My journey includes not internalizing toxic masculinity and continuing to Queer masculinity and participate in my journey of becoming, not assimilating or acquiescing to what is expected of me. Becoming for me is revolutionary and is a revolution of values.

Being more masculine is not necessarily my goal; I am trying to defeminize so that I will present as androgynous, so that I am in/between and both/and. *Soy un Nepantlerx*, a threshold being.

I am a NonBinary Transgender Latinx, and one day soon, I hope to be in my body.

When I recount the story of my body, when I hear the stories of bodies, I wonder if we can embody those stories. I wonder if the narratives of bodies in cages along our southern border disrupt our imagination for what bodies are and how they should be treated. I wonder if story can actually shift the narrative of what embodiment is and give us a vision for democracy when we pair it with embodiment. I believe it can. And I believe that it is in the unknowing and in the motion that we unmask the larger vision for what bodies are.

I am interested in bodies and embodiment and in the complex and complicated connections with ourselves and with one another. I am curious about the kind of relationships we have with one another and how we can shape and shift relationality into a new vision for democracy.

I pose these thoughts to help us get to something like collective liberation. Becoming is not just about self but about self in relationship with others and learning to steward deep enfleshed attachments that can create conditions for our cultural *soma*, our bodies, to move and become the kind of emancipatory world that we long to inhabit.

BODIES AND EMBODIMENT

Clearly, the subjects of bodies and embodiment take up a fair amount of thought space for me—I can't help but think of how fragile our bodies are with illness proliferating, lack of access to medical care for the poor and unhoused, and my own search for competent health care in the South as a Transgender Latinx. I keep coming back to the questions *What bodies count? Who are important?* and *Why does this matter?*

You might feel as though I'm repeating myself in this chapter, and there are elements of repetition, but just like with a clock, each second reveals and reflects a different time. So I invite you into deeper folds of bodies and embodiment. I use the rhetorical device of repetition, inspired by the philosophy of Gilles Deleuze and Félix Guattari. Things might feel repetitive and not as new, and I invite you into that repetition so that the folds can be woven together and you might have a felt sense about why this matters.

Our culture has displaced almost every bit of embodiment for the transactions found within it—largely due to the cultural pain into which we are all conscripted. It's the water in which we are all swimming. How do we survive this deadly terrain? What is our plan? This is not a sprint but a marathon. We've got to be in this for the long game. So how do we survive the tyranny of the now? Especially for this current moment, I continue to ask what a body is and how we manifest new contours of embodiment: How do we feel the pain and suffering that is just below the surface of our skin, the largest organ of our body? How do we participate in the emergence of a felt sense of self? How do we imagine a relationship with our own bodies so that we can become bodied people? With the transactional systems of culture, all of which are supremacist in their insidious logics—and the often disembodied intellectualism of the academy within and feeding culture—I want to go further in my thinking about bodies and embodiment, bringing in story, small vignettes, we together might look at to possibly trace the becoming nature of being (em)bodied.

Requiring time and attention in relating with oneself and with an other, becoming embodied is a process and relationship. I think I often forgot that while growing up in higher education. I experienced the erasure of the body for propositional thinking, a kind of analytic intellectualism that has no pathos and no imagination. It wasn't until I was a wondering nomad in California searching for community as a NonBinary Transgender person that I felt the absence of my body. I could feel the presence of their absence. When we pay attention to our internal processes, it impacts our outer processes, and this allows for a generativity of relationality within ourselves and one another. When we change ourselves, we change how we relate to one another. This process is, I believe, the missing link in fertilizing and harvesting the kind of culture we long for. In many respects, my journey has been like planting a garden and making a way out of no way. I had forgotten how to till my own landscape of becoming and had participated in my own erasure by assimilating into the self-perpetuating elitism of the theological academy.

Not only does culture not privilege some bodies considered other and actively disposes of bodies counted as otherwise or otherworldly, but in its view of bodies, it doesn't privilege the body in any way—we privilege the handheld devices that we carry in our pockets, the little computers that guide our lives. In many ways, an overarching reality of advanced technology has replaced embodiment and has replaced relationship in favor of exploiting transactionality. Technology connects us with our minds while at the same time, perhaps, diminishing our bodies. We favor the brilliant technology of AirPlay and Bluetooth over a tangible relationship and the beauty of shared time at the table. No wonder we have all participated in the erasure of the body. How do we recover ourselves, our materiality, from our own abandonment?

All of us live within this system. None of us are immune to what is happening. In fact, I privilege my iPhone over face-to-face interactions all the time. And living through a global health pandemic, we are all on screens all the time. It's a never-ending and pernicious cycle that separates us from our bodies as well as all the nourishment that comes from the process of becoming bodied.

As a deeply situated introvert, I prefer text over face-to-face interactions because extroverting exhausts me. Perhaps that is why I love writing and contemplative work—yet having people at my table and cooking for them is something I deeply enjoy. It's my love language—and brings together creativity with usually a deeper engagement. Like everyone else, I'm a complex being and am continually trying to understand how different contexts bring something different to embodiedness.

When we begin to make a turn back to the body and really get into all of who we are, we create cultural folds and connections to the becoming process. And the work that Tada Hozumi (among others) is doing to help others turn to the body, to connect neurology to embodiment practices and understand the culture of the West, is very important. Hozumi helps us face and understand the ways that dysregulation impacts our nervous system and thwarts our processes of becoming embodied. Hozumi also helps us understand that ancient practices of the East have been appropriated in the West and accelerate disembodiment. Let me also say that white-bodied folks are so disconnected from their ancestry that they aren't able to access the felt sense of the pain and suffering that often controls them. I am also subject to this dissociative tendency because I've been socialized into whiteness as a mixed-raced Latinx. But we can change that, as Hozumi and others teach. We can change our reality when we lean into an embodied relationality.

The plasticity of the brain and body is made for adaptation—we are made for change. I recall this conversation about the plasticity of the brain and the body when talking with my beloved, Jeff Koetje, in his home in Manhattan. Yet! The ways that inherited thought has shaped our entire cultural body make it difficult to change. It's like our feet are in wet cement. How often have we been talking with our friends or colleagues only to be reminded how deeply our engrained thoughts go? Yet within our bodies is a body's own adaptability, their own desire to change. We have to remember that we are tilling our gardens. We can change our ways; we can change our bodies. We can become (em)bodied beings. Our matter is buoyed by an energetic life force that can be traced back to Indigenous thought. We are alive; we are becoming beings. We have the capacity for changing our entire culture.

White culture privileges the space that white bodies take up, but we are not in our bodies in a complete fashion. It is when we move into our bodies and especially into experiencing feelings in our core or our lower extremities that we are able to get a fuller sense of the bodied moment.

Becoming embodied is about motion, about movement, about the ways that our energetic and generative life force mobilizes the kind of change we want to see in the world.

If we can change ways, bodies, minds, cultures through the adaptability strengthened through embodiment practices, what would happen if we planted this kind of work in our movement circles? What if our churches and faith communities, businesses and schools actually embodied practices that helped reshape our cultural body? What if higher education considered knowledge production beyond the singular lens of cis white males? What would happen if we sought to connect to something other than the data films that occupy each of our brains in their engrained loops? What if we started moving in intentional ways? And what if that movement helped us speak a new kind of language for ourselves? What if that new language helped animate our cultural body in ways profoundly breaking with the dominant system that only speaks in monotone ways? What if we could compost supremacy culture through and by becoming embodied beings?

There's a popular quote from the Afrofuturist writer Octavia Butler that gets to these relationships between bodies and systems: "Everything you touch you change; everything you change, changes you. The only lasting truth is change; God is change." Well, one night, my partner and I talked about this quote. We always share in the cooking and then have deep conversations over farm-to-table food in our home, which we call *La Casa de Somatica*. That night, we had a lovely dinner and wine and decided to enjoy a THC gummy. While we were metabolizing the gummy, we talked about movement and the ways that movement is at the center of everything. Movement is the core of becoming. At one point—and mind you, we were altered at this moment—we were in sync with each other in realizing that movement was at the root of all life.

At that moment, my partner began riffing on the Octavia Butler quote, and these words we now consider a sort of mantra in our house emerged: "All that you touch you move; all that you move moves you; the only lasting truth is movement; God is movement." What if the shaping and shifting of movement facilitate this process of becoming? What if we all realized we need to harness our imagination for movement? What if *movement* is the kind of change we all need to see and feel? And I'm not talking about exercise, though that is a particular kind of movement. I'm talking about a kind of movement rooted in a felt sense. What if we moved from the felt sense of our own materiality? What if that kind of repetitive motion is what accelerated the necessary cultural change that our cultural *soma* needs? What if that is how we save our democracy?

Because our body is composed of millions of other bodies, cultural change is profoundly related to how we frame the concept of a body in the twenty-first century. Can we use our own individual body as an example of what a body is in the twenty-first century? Each cell has a brain, and these brains not only accelerate our being bodied but create pathways for us to connect beyond the materiality of our bodies. These brains are all moving and in concert with movement. Because of the connective relationship of our brain bodies that are contained within our flesh body, we have this as an example of how to actually connect with other bodies, like bodies of culture and society. When we consider becoming embodied as the practice of coming together as not just one body but many bodies, the embodiment process is seen and felt beyond an individual body basis; it is seen and felt and sensed on a collective scale. That can manifest as cultural change!

If becoming is the motion of change we seek, then what if the only lasting change is the becoming movement of who we are to be and become? What if the becoming movement is the not-yet-future for which we all long when we use phrases like "collective liberation"? The not-yet-future is the present that is yet to materialize, but it is moving. What if we learned to dance to the movement that is happening all around us to better participate in the becoming future that we long to inhabit? What if we could feel our way into the future that we are exhaling?

As I pay attention to what is happening around me, I notice so many human creatures seemingly transfixed by their handheld devices, the little computers that help us connect with one another in an ever-expanding global society. Are we just heads floating around with technology attached to us? Are we bodies without organs? Or are we floating systems of thought?

¿Que es un cuerpo? Perhaps a better way to answer the question *What is a body?* is to advance the idea that our felt senses grounded in the body are what allow us to be in relationship with one another, and to be in relationship with one another completes the logic that we must have bodies and we must have a relationship with our bodies. And if we have bodies, we know that our own bodies are connected in some capacity to other bodies through those things built from senses that result in habit and ritual and justice making. We are constantly in motion.

Bodies are systems of *conexiones*, networks of relations that form bonds of trust, and becoming embodied is the process by which they learn the felt senses of their particular systems. Bodies are becoming and are material. Bodies are real, not abstract. Bodies are not floating heads or a collection of displaced organs.

We are deeply connected to the flesh that binds us together, porous and becoming.

And yet embodiment entails other questions.

How do we foster elements of becoming in a world that fragments us into transactions and displaces feeling? How do we destabilize the cultural norms of detached relating informed by relationships of transactions accelerated by and through racialized capitalism?

Sometimes I surprise myself with the questions that bubble up in me, the questions the body asks. Most often I post questions like these on Instagram. Asking them here in this book feels vulnerable. But I know that there is power in getting the truth that lives in my body out. While this is an important question for any body, this question is an important one for me: How do we foster elements of becoming in a world that fragments us into transactions and displaces feeling? How do we learn to participate in the flow of becoming when the world we are in, the water in which we are all swimming, cuts us up into little pieces and disposes of us? I'm exposing my fear and my reality in these questions.

To practice being in my body is something I have had to learn. Literally, I have had to develop a practice. When I turned forty-four during the coronavirus pandemic, I made a commitment to develop a somatic practice—a *soma*, body, practice. It is literally taking a small village to help me get into my body. I now have six embodiment coaches helping me get into my body. And I don't take that lightly. And yet! I am still having a hard time naming my feelings and externalizing the experience of becoming bodied.

Recently, I met with a Chinese medicine practitioner to help me figure out how to deal with some chronic pain I live with due to a condition called adenomyosis, caused by endometrial tissue and often resulting in severe cramps and menstrual bleeding. As I mentioned before, I was assigned female at birth but never identified as female. Nor have I identified as male. Many years ago, I finally came to understand myself as NonBinary Transgender, even as there was no language yet in our culture for those of us who were NonBinary. The language for this kind of embodied orientation slowly developed as we've come to understand gender is not fixed or essential and is actually a socially constructed reality. As I consulted with this Chinese medicine practitioner, we talked about how the uterus is the place of mystery. It made me think of my own work around becoming and the ways in which what I hope is a becoming-being—I want to help us unhinge from systems that lock us down and prevent us from participating in the kind of becoming motion that stewards a better, healthier cultural body.

Being in relationship with all sorts of people, including this Chinese medicine practitioner, is helping me imagine my body and also helping me imagine a process of becoming. My emergent somatic practices include breathing and learning the different parts of the body and the ways that the body is connected and feeling/knowing how it is a whole systemic connection that is related to every part of itself. It has taken almost five years for me to learn the different parts of connectivity with the body: upper-lower, head-tail, core-distal, cross-lateral, and so forth. These are the developmental parts of the body that are mostly referenced in animals, but we have these connections too! I'm still learning all the parts and pieces with work primarily on breathing and developmental movement in order to help me feel. I am still very basic in my somatic understanding; I am not an expert, yet I know that this is what we need to reshape our democracy! It takes time to learn how to unhinge from toxic beliefs and residual trauma that endowed disconnection in my body. We are all conscripted into toxic ideologies and supremacy cultures. And we all have a chance to decode that conditioning and recode our becoming. That process of recoding is in the motion of becoming, the plasticity of positive change—not the mechanistic changes but in literal movement that is connected to networks of relations, grounded in trust.

The materiality of the body—the literal matter we carry with us—is perpetually in the process of change, always becoming. And that is something our body calls us to pay attention to, as our relationship to embodiment also is ever adapting and changing, always becoming. There is motion to becoming.

So do we nurture that process of becoming embodied, or do we displace it for the ways in which the gentrifying ecosystems of varying economies displace and dispose of bodies? That is, do we foster the right relationship with our bodies, or do we leave our bodies, allowing some other technology to care for them?

Capitalism and the overwhelming culture of gentrifying ecosystems seek to colonize our bodies. It's important to pay careful attention to the ways we relate to our bodies—the ones we carry and the bodies around us that make up our cultural body, our cultural *soma*. We all are connected deeply in ways that remain seen and unseen. To participate in the politics of becoming embodied for the sake of creating the kind of world we want to inhabit relies on our commitment to the work of embodiment.

When we listen to stories about the body and the process of becoming, we're helped in imagining both the body we inhabit and the world we want to create. Others' stories and our own—those multiplicities of voices—remind us that becoming is any moment of change and difference and binds us to a process, a relationality of becoming. And embodiment is the ability to feel the edges of our materiality and sense our existence in ways that connect both body and mind as a complete felt sense of being and becoming.

For our cultured bodies, these stories, this conversation of becoming, is important. Many will argue that there is no separation between body and mind, even as we experience how our culture and philosophies have privileged such a separation and have, in fact, built a whole society around the disenfranchisement of the body.

Through narrative and movement, change and plasticity, we begin to retrieve elements of the body so that we can see the relationship of body and mind. My hope is that also through access to the somatic wisdom of different instructors—and my being in deep relationship with the somatics instructor who is my partner—that the work of embodiment that somatics brings will provide another aspect of embodiment that is often left unaddressed in the language of philosophy around embodiment.

Historically, work on the body has been rooted in certain theories, often informed by the dominant culture and most often eclipsing marginalized and minoritized bodies—those otherworldly bodies. Philosophers, feminist theorists, biblical scholars, scientists, theologians, and sociologists, among others, all have contributed to the discourse on bodies. But these contributions have come from a place of objective science or abstraction, with hyperpropositional claims thereby creating a disembodied discourse concerning the body.

Among the first to incorporate the role of experience into theory were the feminist theorists and Queer theorists. With a turn to story—to experience—the body might have a chance to emerge from the weeds of a Cartesian-dominant environment of "I think; therefore, I am." In desperate need of engaging with the felt experience of the *soma*, the body has a chance to express itself through story and memory and experience. When we do, we come close to the cusp of what it means to become embodied. We encounter the motion of becoming. And we get closer still to participating in the vision of democracy, where connection requires the work of becoming, change, and pivoting and shifting out of disembodiment and into becoming an embodied life. I am reminded how much movement is required to get embodied!

In the summer of 2019, when I began writing this book, there were more than 250 mass shootings in the United States. By the end of the year, that number soared to 417—there were more mass shootings in 2019 than there were days. The rate of mass shootings dropped dramatically in 2020, due in large part to the global Covid-19 pandemic that shuttered schools, churches, and virtually all gatherings of any size, public or private. In 2021, however, mass shootings saw a resurgence.

Amid the inundation of violence in 2019, I discovered my own somatic response to the news I read online and in books and magazines. Even in a time of spiritual retreat designed for rest and restoration while I was in the East Bay, California, it was difficult to escape the effects of a 24-hour,

365-days-a-year torrent of terrible news. Even now nausea bubbles up in my body. The dreams that arose are violent; I was at the emperor's whim.

When the violence and the imagination of violence intoxicate our minds and bodies, we suffer. We lose touch with what is True, Good, and Beautiful. Because our bodies are the ground of our thought-body-being, collective social healing will come from our bodies; they are the literal epistemic reality creating conditions for collective liberation. We see how this disembodied violence contributes to the decline of democracy and the decline of a common life that we could share together. How then do our somatic responses contribute to a new level of understanding embodiment?

I want to begin charting this narrative—with bodies as the ground of thought-body-being—as the place where our collective social healing actually can begin to be stitched together, where we can find a way toward liberation and the possibility of democracy, where we can discover a common life when we lean into the movement of becoming embodied.

Bodies are not as elusive as we think them to be. They are resilient and strong, and they hold the stories of our lives. But bodies require gentleness with one another for becoming; they require we listen more deeply to our loved ones, that we, say, cook someone a meal or find ways to offer them a chance to breathe and find respite. I hope we learn to encourage our body's resilience. It takes courage to engage in that work!

We live life by and through bodies. But we don't know how to think through the story of our bodies. In thinking about the story that animates my becoming, I also recall the stories that often have caused me psychic pain, stories that do not facilitate an embodied becoming.

So in asking *What is the body?* Why spend time writing about the stories of the body? Because in story, we see freedom and liberation from the role of the West's domination, we bear witness to the *I* and make a return to the *we*. When we turn toward the *we*, we lean into the imagination of a common life, a life that is becoming, and a vision for a participatory democracy that can create folds of social healing.

When we begin thinking through the lens of connection, we meet belonging and a *we*ness, and we curate a relationality not only with one another but also with our bodies.

The body you have works in dynamic concert and synchronicity to create conditions for your life. In the story of my body, I'm coming to terms with my body and what my body does and does not do. I am also coming to terms with how we have socialized certain bodies into folds of violence. The latter is a kind of embodiment that brews hate, while the former lack of unknowing is attributed to disembodiment.

It is from the body that we learn. We can trace patterns of becoming by learning to listen to the stories of our bodies.

My own story of becoming bodied is riddled with fits and starts. In college, I began to study Tae Kwon Do, and I saw how to discipline the body. Studying this form of martial arts, I disciplined my body, my breath, even my becoming. I don't know if I would say that I was embodied during that time. I had a hard time feeling into my body and was focused more on memorizing the forms and learning how to spar. I wanted to study Tae Kwon Do because I wanted to be stronger and I wanted to be able to defend myself should I be attacked. My immersion into Tae Kwon Do was not from a somatically inspired place, even though I love martial arts and it pointed me to the interconnectivity of the body, the breath, the practice. There is a somatic element to martial arts, though its integrative nature is not often explored in the United States.

When I moved to Chicago for seminary, I began training for century bicycle rides, then later triathlons. Again, I disciplined my body to ride in the saddle for one hundred miles and then learned to swim, bike, and run. I became competitive with myself (something I didn't necessarily love). I was moving but not embodied or bodied in robust ways. When I left Chicago for the PhD program, I stopped moving. After a bout of depression before leaving Chicago, I wanted nothing more than to just sink into the academic study of religion and theology, and that is exactly what I did. I walked away from any kind of movement. I carried so much social anxiety with me as a result of depression that I couldn't ride the bike any longer, and I could no longer tolerate moving like I did when I was on the bike.

My embodiment journey was stunted until I finished my PhD in 2015, when I walked into my therapist's office and told her I want to have a relationship with my body. For me, that was the moment of becoming. It was more than mechanistic change, more than movement of body, more than discipline of the body, which is what the Tae Kwon Do, cycling, and triathlons were. The missing element was that of becoming. The missing element was the relationship between self and body, and in that relationship, I also discovered another aspect of the self—the soul.

III

DIFFERENCE

From the start, let me say this: difference is positive; it is not negative. Philosophically, difference is considered that thing without a norm, even though many often think about difference being *opposite* of something else, possibly even opposite of a norm, where we might say, "This is different than that." The positivity of difference opens up the world to a new and never-receding horizon.

When I use the term *difference*, I am using it much like the philosophical tradition and nonoppositional politics do, where difference illumines a concept or a thought that isn't stable or grounded to a norm.

In the philosophical tradition, the manner in which ideas emerged and were explored was within a framework of identity, opposition, analogy, and resemblance, where each formed one of the four pillars of reason. And difference has been subordinated to these pillars. For our purposes, we'll be envisioning difference along a plane of thinking and thought production that does not reduce difference to negation but rather elevates it to something positive and emerging, not in contrast to something else but in relationship to something else. Difference is about connection and connecting, not about opposing. Difference is a good thing, and when we harness an imagination composed of difference, we can shape and shift our world. Gloria Anzaldúa called this *la naguala*. And *la naguala* is an effort to shape and shift through practices of resistance and generative subjectivities. *La naguala* embodies the politics of radical difference to resist the bullshit of the tyranny of the now and shape the world we long to inhabit.

THE JOURNEY TO BECOMING EMBODIED

In 2015, when I moved to California, I found a therapist and told her I wanted to "get into my body." She was a white woman, and I was not confident that she would be able to help me, but six years later, we continue to meet for our weekly sessions, and I am amazed at how she bridges together cultural awareness of my mixed-raced body and challenges me to knit together an embodied life. I didn't know what that meant then, and I am still on a journey for what it means now. I am always becoming. *Poco a poco.*

Being bodied, as I like to think about it, is directly related to becoming, that sometimes by a realization of inertia, we begin to want to move and feel or are compelled to move and feel. That motion and movement that are the only lasting truths of our being are what I've been metabolizing for the last five years to get to a place where I have a relationship with my body.

There are 150 acres of land at Penuel Ridge Retreat Center, just outside of Nashville in Ashland City, Tennessee, where the land is stewarded with peace, love, and justice. And in 2020, I went on a retreat there, knowing I wanted to be on that land as I was writing this book so that I could feel more deeply into my self—feel the land's texture between my toes and breathe in the ancestry of what has been there. One afternoon I took a hike and found Lake Joyce. I sat down on the bench near the lake, took off my shoes, and just let myself feel the ground beneath me; I tried to feel into connection. This is a thing that people do—it's called *earthing*. They feel into the earth—something I longed to experience. It was seventy-five degrees that day, and the sun was beautiful, beaming down on me. I was wearing a tank and some cotton pants. Because of the way my brain works, living with autism, it's hard for me to wear socks and shoes. I like to go barefoot as much as I'm able, so it felt really nice to have my feet fully connected to the earth. (My partner loves to go earthing, and my embodiment coaches all encourage me to go earthing every chance I get.)

After several minutes on the bench, I put my shoes back on and continued along the path in search of the labyrinth that I was told was there on the property. To find it, I had to get moving and search for it! I love labyrinths. They are mesmerizing to me. I often feel as though I am in a trance when I walk them. I have a dear friend with whom I walk labyrinths when we are together and we find one. Once I found the labyrinth, I again took off my shoes and began to walk its path. As I was walking, I began to just let myself feel into the ground. It was damp and cool, and I was beginning to feel a buzz in my body. Now, I don't know if that was a connection point between the earth and myself, but it certainly felt as if I was connecting to something beyond myself. At one point in the walk, a leaf landed on my tank, near my stomach. I looked at the leaf and felt connected anew to the trees around me, feeling as though they were taking care of me, the leaf a messenger of that care. It felt as if all that was and is ensouled—the ground stewarded in justice and the trees surrounding me ushering me through this path of the labyrinth, like a doula, and helping me connect. Now, just to be clear, I'm a five on the Enneagram—not too spiritual. In fact, I tell people that I am more religious than spiritual because I have habits that help me feel secure. Yet in all of this, I think the world has a spirit of animism—that all things are alive and endowed with Spirit—but I'm not an overly spiritual or emotional person, so to have this experience felt as though I was a little closer to a somatic experience, that felt sense I had been cultivating all these years in therapy. I felt the radical interconnectedness of all things. I felt as though the world was holding me with a fierce tenderness and helping me see more clearly why embodiment is a vision for a new democracy and democratic justice.

Coming to this place of connection after all the work that I had done over the last five years was a wonderful feeling. Becoming is not just change; it is the relationship we have to flux and change, to pivots and the wrinkles in time. What I was able to experience on that hike and walking the labyrinth that fall day was the process of becoming embodied.

I was in relationship with the earth, and my body was in connection with the ground, which was facilitating a much larger bodily connection. I felt different; I felt changed; I felt the motion of becoming.

The more I feel into my body, the more I realize how disconnected I've been and the more I learn what it's meant to live on the autism spectrum. Among the stories of the trauma I experienced and how I've come to understand myself as Transgender, there is another story: how I was taught to suppress my pain rather than address it. My white father always thought I was "crying wolf" whenever I expressed discomfort, the feeling of any sort of pain. I recall tripping and falling onto a rock so hard that the rock, lodged into the ground, dented my leg—a dent my leg still wears. Those experiences were the seeds of my disembodied life, the tragedy, as I think about it now. I always felt as though he was playing a joke on me, but then I came to realize that his minimizing my pain and suffering was part of his own internalized pain and suffering. We are victims of our ancestral pain.

Perhaps he didn't have the capacity to care for me. Perhaps he didn't understand that pain was an element of strength. Whatever it was, I learned from a very young age how to suppress my pain and live a fragmented life. This reality is something I see played out on a cultural level too. It is not just a singular moment reduced to an individual; we have created a cultural body that is expected to suppress pain and grief and internalize trauma instead of process and metabolize these elements. We are the cultural body that we are because of unprocessed trauma. We are not only disembodied; we are disconnected from ourselves, one another, the planet, the animals, and all living life.

I always wanted to feel as though I was fully myself. I didn't understand until recently that getting into my body and learning to have a relationship with my body was part of learning who I am and becoming my full self. As an academic, I've taken many different journeys with the mind, but not so with the body. I'm on a journey now to become closer with my own materiality, my own body, so that I can not only heal what is wounded within me but learn to be the healing of the wounds of the world. It's my vision for a participatory democracy and democratic justice.

The healing of the world has motivated me to seek embodiment help. I have wanted to know how to heal our culture and create a culture shift. I've never had a tweet go viral, and considering it now, I think it's largely because I want to be in relationship with people, not be a megaphone for people to listen to. Relationships will save us, but it's the kind and quality of those relationships that will save us. And proximity to relationship is what invites more embodied relationship, not 280 characters going out into the ether that people like or retweet. That's not going to save our society. It's relationships all the way down for me.

Relationships, though, done well and from an embodied place, have the potential to create conditions for healing. That's why I'm on this journey, and that's why I have taken the longer route to become embodied, to learn to participate in healing our culture.

* * *

Some of the stories of embodiment that have been formative for me have provided different understandings for me
and have informed this book, as the journey of embodiment is never alone but always in relation to. As I've been
writing this book, I've invited people to share their stories of embodiment and the healing of the world. I share
some of their stories in this chapter. Among them is
Dr. Jaime Beuerlein's (she/they) story of embodiment and
how she learned to displace the hegemonic powers that con-
script us all with the becoming potential of embodiment.

Jaime has had to—and continues to—fight for her
embodiment. She was raised and socialized as a male in the
model of "manhood" we now call toxic masculinity. She's
also white. The culture of her family led her to believe that
displays of emotion were a sign of weakness. Ironically, this
message came most predominantly from her mother, who
lost both of her parents at a young age and her first hus-
band to a tragic accident. The only way her mother learned
to cope was by suppressing her own emotions. She saw it
as an absolute necessity to survival. She expected Jaime
and her siblings to develop the same stoic "strength" and
detachment. She even remarked at one point that she had a
hard time making friends with peers because she couldn't
tolerate anyone who was "too emotional." For her, feeling
was a character flaw—one that she did her best to hammer
out of Jaime.

As a child, Jaime had a phobia of calling strangers on
the phone. The idea of calling an unknown adult, whom

she couldn't see, terrified her. What if she mixed up her words? Or froze? What if they got mad? Her mother would force her to make calls—through her tears—to friends' parents, the pizzeria for delivery, the post office, and so on. She believed that forced exposure therapy would rid Jaime of her fears and give her intellectual mastery over her weaker (read "emotional") tendencies. When Jaime was afraid of the dark, she'd be forced to sit in the crawl spaces of the barn in pitch-black darkness. Afraid of big, loud, dangerous machines, she was forced to operate tractors, bailers, lawnmowers, and the like beginning at age ten. And her punishments were corporal, so she learned to deny pain in her body as well.

She learned that emotional expression was inherently unsafe in the context of her family; her Christian church taught her that her "flesh" was evil and that the body was sinful and would ultimately perish—allowing her soul to finally escape the source of its torment. The one-two punch of faith and family was the reason it took Jaime three and a half decades to finally admit she was Transgender.

She writes,

As my theological framework slowly disintegrated, it was replaced by a sensitivity and an unwavering certainty in the goodness and dignity of every human life—regardless of background, creed, origin, sex, color, or body. Even then, an intellectual assent to the goodness of others was slow to transform into believing that my body is good. That she is good.

Personifying her and giving her the appropriate pronouns was an earth-shattering shift in my perception of self. My body is not an "it"; she is a "her."

The story of my journey into embodiment would not be complete if left in isolation. The truth is that every body—my body—affects and is affected by the bodies we come into contact with. Embodiment is social as well as personal. Having been raised and socialized as a male—and being white—left me at the apex of privilege and unexamined supremacist ideology. My journey into self quickly made me aware of the effect of my body on those around me. As a thirty-year-old white doctor and a man, I assumed primacy. Entitlement and superiority were the water I swam in. If anyone had asked, I would have said that I was color-blind and saw women as equal but different. The reality was, however, that I had not examined how the supremacy culture of cisgender, heterosexual, white males had both privileged and disembodied me. How the very qualities I was now striving to possess (femininity and emotional fluency) had been weaponized by people who looked like me to oppress and invalidate women, the LGBTQ+ community, and people of color. Upon coming out as Transgender, I learned for the first time what it meant to have my body seen by that same supremacist culture as bad, as wrong, as a threat.

I cannot say that I have "arrived" at a more evolved consciousness. I can say that it has been my journey into my body that has humbled me, that has revealed my privilege, and that motivates me to work toward ongoing internal (as well as social) change. I am grateful for the opportunity I have been given to relearn my humanity. I am grateful for the lives of the men, women, and gender-nonconforming siblings whose bodies have paved the way for me to awaken. The work is hard. The fight is necessary.

Another person whose story and whose work for embodied healing have been profound for me is Kate Moore (she/her), my personal trainer in embodiment, compassion, and body movement and the body's capacity. Kate has helped me love my body and in turn helped me accept others loving my body. I am indebted to Kate for her work with me as she continues to companion me with my becoming body.

Kate describes herself as "a nondisabled, neurotypical, middle-class, cis white woman in this world" who suddenly found herself in the industry of fitness and wellness in her twenties. She's said "all of the surface-y inspirational bullshit that you'll likely hear in most wellness spaces without context or understanding" and began to understand the inherent harm in not telling the whole truth. She learned that the body-positivity movement wasn't enough. It doesn't work to just "let it go and be happy." It doesn't work to just "love yourself." She began to ask the next question:

But then what? What about when you still don't see your body or perspective or culture represented in a positive way out in the world? Because it's not just that you don't see yourself; it's that other people don't see us in a positive way either—and those unintentional beliefs + implicit biases become the way we see and function in the world. We make judgments, rules, technology, and entire societies based on these biases—this is the beginning of systemic harm. Because "loving yourself" isn't enough within a system that is built to remind you that you aren't "it." The systems are powered by our labor and our bodies—not by our inherent human dignity, our uniqueness, or our communities. So we go home at night, lay our heads on our pillow, and remember that time our thin white yoga teacher told us to "let it go" and wonder why it's so hard to just let it go. . . . Wow, what a shame spiral. What if, instead of "let it go," we valued understanding what's here instead.

Her journey toward embodiment, she says, has had its ups and downs. She's grown to understand her body and her "Being" more deeply and more honestly and also has grown to understand the world more deeply and more honestly. Her capacity for "yes, and" has deepened, allowing her to hold humanness more freely and more lovingly: "The flaws, the harm, the biases, and the misunderstandings alongside and with the dignity, goodness, capacity for growth, and capacity for both great love and great violence, intentional or unintentional, that each of us inhabits. This journey toward embodiment has taken the world from being a black or white place to being colorful, Queer, Black, white, and any blend of the in-between place." She reflects on the longing for a feeling of freedom in her body, and yet the growing demands from society and capitalism to produce feel endless and perpetually exhausting. As her body pleads with her to slow down, she also recognizes the need to be present and actionable in our collective fight toward freedom that she says "is absolutely necessary and imperative that we continue":

> This capacity has come and gone in big waves. When there's an honest embodiment of anger and courage, I feel energized, clear, directional, and intentional. This anger can also come with a sense of urgency, control, and overwhelm. The urgency, control, and overwhelm seem to come when I need rest and space because often when I ask my anger what's fueling her, her answer is that she's afraid, alone, and feeling out of control. Sometimes the anger needs movement—for me, this sometimes looks like picking up heavy things or jumping up and down or just screaming as loudly as I can from deep within my belly. From there, I can have a conversation with the fear. I can tell her, "Thank you for being with me" and "I know you are trying to keep me safe" because that has value. I can also tell her firmly and kindly, "You can stay here in my body if you need to, and I will be moving forward with intention and clarity—you will not keep me stuck."

She writes about finding capitalism and systemic racism and oppression "a fully disembodied reality," systems that exist and systems we are not fully able to live without. Frustration often exists in her body because of this, a feeling of being out of control, a tightness in her throat, an elevated rhythm of her heart, and repetitive neurological thoughts that seem to be attempting to solve this confusing and frustrating challenge. "While we cannot escape from what *is*," she explains, "we also must not allow what IS to be all that we can imagine for ourselves, for society, for future generations, and for our earth":

We live in a society of systems here in America that keeps us from understanding ourselves, our bodies, our stories, and our patterns. These systems keep us from understanding our way of being in the world. That's powerful to recognize: because when we don't understand ourselves, it's extremely challenging to understand the systems of power that are constantly impacting our lives *and* it's extremely challenging to understand ourselves without understanding the systems that currently exist.

Embodiment is both a personal practice and teamwork. No one can do it for us, and we can't force anyone to join us. It's a choice, a practice, a calling. It takes courage to be honest about ways in which you've been hurt as well as ways in which you've hurt others. It takes courage to grow. It takes courage to change the systems. It's individual on every level, and it's communal on every level too.

When I consider "What does freedom feel like in my body?" the overwhelming answer is just "truth." Freedom feels like telling the deepest most challenging truth. Freedom feels like not holding on for dear life. Freedom feels *complete.* Freedom feels like a deep knowing. I've learned that this knowing doesn't come from my thinking brain—it's not a voice that comes in. It's a voice that comes up—as if my body is putting words to truth, not my brain.

When Moore reflects on how you, the reader, might engage the work of embodiment and begin that invitation with the book you are holding in your hands, the words, the explorations, she brings her own words from training, from personal embodiment work:

I hope that you invite your body into this book. Invite your body to have an experience with this book. I invite you to jump around the next time you feel angry—not to end the anger, but to find clarity with the anger. To put a hand on your heart when you are hurting—not to stop the hurt from being there, but to care for it as long as it needs to stay. To feel into the truth that you are loved the next time you are feeling alone—not to end the current experience of loneliness, but to hold the truth of being loved alongside the impermanent experience of loneliness. To breathe deeply into the depths of your belly the next time you forget who you are or why you're here—because, if you're paying close attention to the vastness of this life experience, sometimes the importance of your existence may get lost, and in my experience, the depths of your body have a way of reminding us of our life, our breath, our very existence. Perhaps there's no answer to "Why do we exist?" but only the conundrum that we do.

After all, all bodies are inherently good bodies. What does that feel like?

Gert Comfrey (they/them/theirs) works as a licensed marriage and family therapist. In their work with others, they help people consider arriving into and attuning to their body, something that will continue to be a lifelong process.

"In a world plagued by systemic oppression, disembodiment is the posture encouraged by cisheteronomativity and patriarchy, capitalism and classism, white supremacy and colonialism, ableism and ageism," they write. "These systems, all of which work together, are designed to keep us in states of disconnection from our bodies so that those very systems of oppression can flourish and self-perpetuate." They understand that these systems are designed to keep us silent and literally cut off from our own voices and therefore complicit, systems of oppression designed to keep us out of alignment with incredibly powerful sources of wisdom—our own bodies.

The story of systems of oppression in the body is something Gert has felt; their own body has been a site of oppression. They have felt the demand from capitalism to dissociate away from their body's exhaustion and to continue selling their labor for the benefits of the owning class. They have felt the demand from white supremacy "to ignore and invalidate the angry racing of [their] heartbeat when [they] bear witness to institutionalized racism." They have felt the demand from cisheteronormativity to repress and exile into the shadows the longings in their body to love and express. They have felt the demand from ableism to criticize, discard, or fix their body "for the ways it fails to meet the oppressively narrow criteria of what constitutes a good body." Under these systems of oppression, they have been encouraged to have a fractured relationship with their body "in service of these very systems." Reflecting on the interrelated and interlocking systems of oppression, Gert points to what it means for the body to wear each of the demands, the oppressions, the expectations of the systems. "How insidious," Gert responds, "how dehumanizing, how traumatizing."

There are many ways bodies in systems like these respond, and Gert begins here:

I must resist. Just as I resist oppressive systems on the institutional and interpersonal levels, so too must I resist them on the intrapersonal and embodied levels. For me, resistance means reclaiming my body as my own from the clutches of internalized oppression. It means acknowledging that under these systems, I am in a constant struggle against the wounds of dismemberment and aim to move toward my own re-membering. It is a process of calling back home to myself with radical hospitality all of the parts of me, including bodily sensations, movements, memories, and intuitions, that were once exiled, silenced, and marginalized. It is literally me remembering who I am on a cellular and genetic level, in spite of systems demanding that I not. It is the work of abolition, the dismantling of oppression and the building up of liberating alternatives.

And in the building process, I am comforted by the reminder that another world is possible. Another world inside my body, an alignment deeply tuned into wisdom, intuition, and liberation, is possible. I get glimpses of it regularly.

Gert moves their liberated body in participation with Neon Guard, a people's safety team in Nashville, Tennessee. The team actively puts their bodies between police (and other threats) and marginalized communities. In those moments, Gert says, "I have felt my body come alive, feeling a deep sense of connection to my humanity and alignment with what I feel in my gut is right and true: all marginalized communities deserve space to express themselves without fear of violent retaliation."

> I settle into my liberated body when I allow the binary between body and mind to dissolve and when I honor my body as a source of deep wisdom of what liberation itself looks and sounds and feels like. My body tells me when I am in spaces where I can breathe deeply and freely, where I can soften my gut, where my tears are welcome, where my whole humanity is honored in its sacredness.
>
> Here, my deeply wise animal body begins to remember a time before domestication and the exile of all that is wild. Here, play and passion and desire and pleasure are celebrated for what they are. I can tune into the true pace of my body, which is very, very slow. And I can root more firmly into the profound goodness and wholeness of my body, knowing that all bodies are good bodies. I can tune into what is truly nourishing for my body, including food, the company I keep, and the places I go. I can trust my intuition and channel my energies exactly where they need to flow.

As Gert roots their body, as they keep pace with their own embodiment, as they understand embodiment as essential for resistance against systems of oppression and the direct action of putting their being between systems of oppression and those marginalized by systems, Gert acknowledges what the body feels in and beyond those moments: "And there is pain in moving toward my liberated body," they write. "But rather than the oppressive pain of disembodiment, this pain is one of growth and transformation. This pain reminds me that trauma lives in my body, both my own as well as that of my ancestors. I carry within my body generations; I do indeed contain multitudes." Gert tends to what they call "the grief altar of my body" as healing is being channeled to their body, to the bodies of others, both to the past and to the future.

In a body placing itself in resistance, in grief, in transformation, Gert knows their survivor body to be resilient, a body that, they write, "speaks to [them] daily in images, metaphors, flashes of memories, sensations, pain, tears, screams, movement and dance, song and sound." Gert writes, "My body is a portal, an oracle I approach with curiosity and humility. Being deeply in my body means having access to my sacred yes and my strong no and any nuance I allow in between. I hold sacred the canvas of my Queer body for genuine expression and celebration." Their body, their altar of grief from past to future, their body between is also a body related to other bodies, human and plant bodies. "Here, I'm also reminded that my body is a fractal of our parent planet," they write. "The microcosm of my body contains her four elements: earth and minerals in my bones, water in my blood and cells, air flowing within my lungs, and fire burning at around 98.6° Fahrenheit." Their body is "beloved of Earth, inherently, intrinsically, completely. . . .

Recovering and reclaiming my body is my forever work. For me, the process of unfolding into my body and its wisdom has implications on personal, interpersonal, systemic, institutional, and political levels. In an oppressive world banking on my continued disembodiment, I resist by dropping deeply into embodiment and daring to access liberation."

In these stories, I see shape-shifting possibility, resistance to the tyranny of the now, and composting the bullshit that keeps us disconnected and unable to imagine another possible world. It is in the telling of our stories and *restorying* ourselves into an embodied life that we taste the contours of liberation on a collective scale. These stories embody the kind of possible and participatory democracy that we need.

A well-worn psalm from the Hebrew Bible is one I also return to often (as I'll do in a later chapter), that "people perish without a vision." These stories help us create a vision forward into the folds of embodiment. It's a path that is both personal and social, requiring a kind of moral courage at every step on the path that creates conditions for us to say "Yes, and . . ."

When we have the kind of embodied agency to say "Yes, and . . . ," we come into greater awareness of what's possible with our bodies. We learn that we can be agents of change and agents of resilience instead of just continuing along the path of being conscripted into supremacy culture.

We actually need story to narrate change, and we need the ability to restory ourselves to embody resistance to the kinds of mechanisms that tether us to a disembodied and dystopian life. The future is a future of embodiment, a future of the never-receding horizon of difference, and I can feel the warm illumination of that future becoming.

BODIES, VIOLENCE, AND EMBODIMENT

I want to start by talking about violence against bodies so that we have a fuller picture of the work that needs to be done. Because embodiment relies so heavily on whether we can cultivate a relationship with our bodies, I want to write about those things that make us tremble, shut us down, get us squeamish, get us running. That also means I need to rush in with content and trigger warnings because we all have nervous systems, and our nervous systems all function differently. I'll be recounting violence and the impact of that violence on my person and body. I've limited the details to this chapter only. All of us have triggers, and maybe the best thing—for me, for you, for us and our bodies—is to simply remind us all of a good exercise to do when we hear words like *trigger, warning, tremble*: I invite you to pause and perhaps also breathe.

As I started to write this chapter, my Apple Watch chimed and reminded me to breathe. I stopped and breathed for one minute. My body is smart, even if it is neuroatypical. Here's to resilience! Here's to finding conditions for thriving in a world that only wants to cut me up into little pieces. Did my Apple Watch notice an increase in my heart rate as I was preparing to write this chapter? I'll never know, but I'm learning to trust my body anew each and every day.

So what transpired in my body that prompted my watch to chime and have me breathe? My favorite author would say that it was a spirit and being on sacred land—again, I'm writing at Penuel Ridge—there is a spirituality to this place. So I don't know what it was exactly, but my body is smart, and I'm glad this is an instance where technology listens to my body and not the other way around. I took a chance to breathe and stop for a moment. Our bodies have an intelligence that supersedes logic, even those bodies that are nonneurotypical. Part of my neurodiversity is my body's intelligence. I was able to respond with a connective response, which was to breathe. And even as I write into those stories that require content warnings, I am reminding myself and you as well, breathing helps.

In August 2017, I was invited to Charlottesville, Virginia, to participate in an opposition against the Unite the Right rally, a rally for white supremacy. I was invited there to provide an embodied presence of difference and resistance, and so I went. But at that rally, I saw the ways in which different bodies—bodies of difference—were treated, creating anxiety and concern in me and my own body of difference.

When I arrived, I had lots of questions. Was I safe to walk around? Would the alt-right target me? I had all these questions circling in my mind, and I worked to be centered in my body during this time, but with all that transpired in Charlottesville, I found it difficult to remain grounded in my body and in the wisdom of what my body offers me.

There I walked with the Reverend Traci Blackmon and with Clinton Wright, our security detail for this event. When we arrived and parked the car, Traci advised me not to put on my clerical stole because, she said, it was unsafe. My stole has "Black Lives Matter" in clear letters, and my stole is bright red, so it is very noticeable. The energy was tense; I still remember it in my body, and even upon returning home to Nashville, my body was buzzing because it was on high alert. But I truly learned the answers to these questions—*What is a body? Whose bodies count?*—when I stood on the corners of Second and Water Streets that fateful day. What I did not know at the time was that my body would continue to be targeted by these right-wing ideologues long after I left Charlottesville and still to this day.

Soon after I returned home, I began receiving Twitter messages and emails, and unmarked packages slowly began arriving at my doorstep. Someone had my address and was mailing packages in an effort to scare and harass me. My body felt threatened and I knew this was not the way we should be treating one another. This was not a vision for democracy. My body has intelligence; every body has intelligence. And my body was absorbing this hate in ways that continue to impact me. My sleep was affected, my anxiety was palpable, and I struggled to make sense of all that was transpiring. I even had to move from that house to be more secure. Because I didn't want my roommates at the time to be impacted, I didn't tell them why I was moving.

As I waded through hate mail and packages sent to my home, I began to think about the kind of world we want to build. What is our collective vision? What does it look like, and how do we build it? Not through scare tactics and fear, I said out loud to myself, but through the gentle and fervent ways of being kind with one another, by practices of radical folds of hospitality and generosity. Such generativity breeds a relationality of kindness, which begins to shape and shift both embodiment itself and the vision for the kind of humanity we want to embody. These practices of kindness have the potential to create an environment of togetherness—and, I really like to think, that sense of togetherness can actually reshape our culture. As I like to say to those who lean into this work, *Somos en conjunto.*

Embodiment is key. Bodies are key. We can't shift the future in the direction we want it to go without first shifting our cultural understandings of bodies. This work demands our attention to self and attention to other—and the relationship between self and other, nurtured between our individual selves and our cultural self, actually creates tangible change.

The farther away I got from the events at Charlottesville, the more I thought about bodies and embodiment. Soon the immigration situation along the southern border of the United States emerged as a national crisis.

Daily, my body felt the new cataclysms, controversies, or outrage—whether real or manufactured—diverting our attention and energy from the work of embodiment and creating the kind of world we want to embody. Yet the crisis at the southern border actually is central to my body in relationship with our democratic body and our work of embodiment.

I began to ask additional questions. How are we treating these bodies at the border? Do we welcome the stranger? What is our vision for who our neighbor is? And to explore what this looks like locally, how do we create neighborhoods that are not products of disaster capitalism and actually are environments for all bodies to thrive and flourish?

As I ponder such questions, I recall how my family crossed borders to get to where they are now. Immigration is no easy thing, and our system is not set up to make it easy. I worry about border crossers and how they are oftentimes victims of theft, rape, and even death. Years ago, when I walked the migrant trails carrying jugs of water for those I might encounter along the way, I remember seeing places migrants would stop to pray, where they built makeshift altars as they struggled to make a safe passage; they relied on the kindness of strangers and fellow migrants to ensure their safety. And I also saw where the US Border Patrol slashed water jugs and emptied them, making certain there were no resources available along the trails. I knew then that we aren't living in the kind of world many of us long to inhabit. And my body could feel the struggle that my own family endured as they migrated from Oaxaca, Mexico, to Nuevo León, Mexico, and northward. The movement of migration is ongoing and, for many, never ending.

Walking the migrant trails was humbling. Even just the physical terrain can be treacherous. The Arizona desert can be deadly for those without appropriate shelter and resources, and I'll be the first to tell you that I am not built for the kind of weather that proliferates in the desert. The two nights I spent in a tent in the desert were so cold, I worried about hypothermia. The first night, my body felt a kind of fatigue and cold I never experienced before, and I even had a sleeping bag that would keep me warm in below-zero temperatures; still, I was very cold that night. The next night, our group had access to a heater—a privilege the vast majority of migrants walking the trails would never have. I spent a lot of time wondering whether I would move my sleeping bag closer to the heater or not. I was too cold, though, so I did!

Our country, motivated by white Christian religious nationalism, is creating the kind of policies that force migrants to endure the desert, and these policies are killing my kin. I want to embody what it is to build a different world; I want us to compost our bullshit and truly steward a conversation around cultural pain. I want us to be free from multisystem oppressions. And creating and embodying this vision will, I know, also require us to process our cultural pain and regulate our systems for the health of all bodies in our culture to enable us to be human with one another. We need embodiment to do this; we need bodies to do this.

We need to be appalled at the ways our immigration policies enforce violence against bodies, separation from families and relational bodies, and sometimes death. If we are
not appalled, then we are not in touch with our own suffering and dissociative realities. We need to get in touch
with our ancestral pain and suffering so that we can connect with the current wounds and suffering around us. If
we don't, then we won't be embodying the necessary tools
to shape and shift our cultural pain and our cultural soma.

On the migrant trails, a person has to figure out where to
use the bathroom and eliminate their waste. During the
time I spent walking the trails with the group No More
Deaths / No Más Muertes, I was privileged to use a five-
gallon bucket to eliminate my waste. I remember sitting on
a very cold toilet seat overlooking the desert as I began to
release the waste from my body. I felt the chills from the toilet seat, but I also felt incredibly free. There I was, a Transgender person sitting on an improvised toilet in the open
desert—I could feel the gravity of what that meant. I have
been kicked out of bathrooms in the past, so I carry with me
bathroom anxiety. But not that day. Though I encountered
cold and chills, in that moment, my body was able to do
what it needed to do, free from harm, even in the midst of
this harsh, arid place.

Rarely are those who walk the migrant trails as lucky as I
was. I have citizenship, even though I am marked differently
as a gendered person. The trails tell a story of violence and
hardship, one that members of my family endured before
me, and some of my family—namely, my mother—face

hardship and ridicule due to the color of their skin to this day. The trails also are a holy place. They hold the people who travel and the rituals they do before they die from the struggle of migration or before they finally cross over and get to a safe space by being both a welcoming and treacherous place. I recognized the migrant trails as also a place where embodiment happens. I felt my own body changing while I was walking those trails. What would I say to a migrant if I happened upon them? My group would shout out that we had water, but we didn't encounter anyone that day.

The migrant trails inspire questions about who are we becoming, questions for all of us to ask whether we're walking the trails or not:

What kind of humans do we want to become?
What kind of world are we seeking to inhabit?

Embodiment answers such questions. But we don't yet know how we become embodied. We don't yet know how to steward the kind of connection and relationship with our selves that will result in an embodied living that can chart the kind of social courage in the people who will build the world we long to inhabit. Do we have the social courage to lean into this kind of work?

How can we create conditions for social courage?
Do we have a vision for social courage?

In a world where in our politics, bodies are written out in favor of policies that either erase certain bodies and privilege others or completely negate some bodies in the first place, embodiment is a centralizing, interrelational question, whether we are talking about immigration or gender discrimination or who gets police "protection" on Charlottesville streets.

What happens when we begin to reclaim bodies and lean into the work of becoming embodied?

How does this particular work reshape relationships and our understandings of relationality?

Our world and our culture promote and accelerate violence against bodies. Our embodiment is threatened by policies and politics that don't have regard for the felt sense of the body or for the ways our feelings and emotions are impacted by all that is happening in the world. So the question about reclaiming our bodies and leaning into the work of becoming embodied is also about how we care for ourselves and learn to care for one another.

With manifold violence occurring at our borders and with a global pandemic creating the violence of cascading grief, it is important to think through and feel through how to be as present with our selves and with one another as best as we can, asking the following questions: What are our practices of being present? Are we breathing with our collective body, or is our collective body so broken and in pain that we cannot access the collective nature of our body? Presence first begins with us, with me. And after me, it begins with the *I* connected to the *we*, and we must find a way to stitch together the broken pieces of our becoming and suture our wounds that stem from the personal out to the political.

Writing in a pandemic, I witnessed the growing awareness of loss and grief during a time with little to no support
in our government, including state government. And I am
now writing in a current moment of uprisings that emerged
during the spring and summer. I wonder how we steward
the kind of world we long to inhabit.

When we are entrenched in unhelpful power dynamics, such as minimizing the impact of our current moment
on marginalized bodies, we end up being in an unhealthy
relationship with power. I write about violence in relationship to bodies because we must have a power analysis
of what is happening in these moments. Embodiment
emerges when we have a trustworthy relationship with our
bodies and are able to steward a felt sense of our bodies.
Violence encourages the wrong kind of world, a world that
creates conditions for violence against bodies instead of
one that seeks to suture the cultural pain and create conditions for bodies to exist without the threat of violence.

At that Charlottesville Unite the Right rally, I could actually feel the hate toward my body and the indifference to
marginalized people. There was a tangible feeling in the
air, an environment lacking welcome and hospitality. It
felt as close to me as my own breath. Reflecting on that
experience, I am aware that our felt sense also is tied to
the cultural body—that is, our social practices are tied
to our bodies, and embodiment emerges from that particular
relationship. When I watched militia men, neo-Nazis, and
other right-wing men bearing signs and weapons at that
rally, I understood that their embodied action was also tied

to the cultural body. Violence is not just an isolated event but a larger symptom of the violence enacted within our cultural body.

In the evenings in my residence in Nashville, I sometimes hear gunshots, and I realize that they are not isolated to the community in which they are fired. The gunshots are connected to a larger problem of historic and cascading violence that prevents communities from being connected through embodied solidarity. The gunshots point back to power and the toxic environments beyond this community that unhealthy relationships with power and control breed.

Environments of crisis also inhibit our ability to be embodied. There are so many concerns present in our world—so many of us are hustling to keep a roof over our heads and food on our table that we turn to an orientation of living that doesn't steward embodiment but rather stewards more scarcity and disconnection from communities, inhibiting our ability to be embodied. In our current reality, how do we foster from crisis something that has conditions for embodied living? Seeing how we can shift culture and create conditions for a better world to emerge and a better body politic to generate folds of cultural healing requires addressing the overwhelming reality of cultural trauma and pain that prevents a connection and felt sense with our bodies, including our cultural body. I think about how isolation actually impacts our cultural body and promotes further disconnection.

Trauma is one of the things that we all have in common. And unprocessed trauma proliferates in our society and creates systems of oppression, like racism. In our culture, we can trace racism back to its roots of being white-on-white violence and unhealthy relationships with power and control. White-on-white violence is part of our inherited cultural trauma and pain and extends itself to being white violence toward anything or anyone that doesn't adhere to the structures of white violence. This, too, impacts our ability to be embodied, especially when all we know is violence.

Our response to people who think differently from us often is an us-versus-them mentality, which is rooted in the colonial logic of divide and conquer. This, too, is violent and establishes more white-on-white violence, since many folks who would call themselves progressives or liberals tend to attack and react to those who hold to another side of an issue. This is not only dangerous but also a fold of supremacy culture we condone because we justify it, saying the GOP and Republicans are so awful. That kind of logic isn't valuable, nor will attacking the other side that doesn't agree with you create conditions for healing our wounds. Neither side forwards the logic of liberation. We need a new vision for politics, government, and democracy.

Attacks, reactions, and white-on-white violence only deepen our shared conscription into supremacy culture. When we choose relationship and connection over attacks and disconnection, we shift not only the culture of whiteness, which is rooted in disconnection and fragmentation, but the ways in which we are in relationship to and with trauma, especially the unprocessed trauma that perpetuates systemic oppression. Oppression exists because we've policed imagination out of peoples and communities. As my academic partner, Dr. Nikki Young, said years ago, "Imagination is the best thing we have on our sides."

We are socialized into a framework of violence that fortifies a relationality of disembodied living. When we build communities and cultures from this place of disembodied living, we sustain more cultural pain and unresolved trauma. When we actively work against the ways in which we are socialized and confront the violence with empathy and compassion, we begin to shift our cultural responses, helping create conditions for a healthier cultural body to emerge.

I have grown up around a lot of violence of different types, which has impacted me as an individual and as a person living in society. What I know is this: Bodies deserve a chance to have a felt sense instead of being in cycles of trauma—always freezing, fleeing, fighting, or collapsing in a world that does not steward embodied connection. Bodies deserve bridged difference. Stewarded connection.

We have inherited theologies, ethics, policies, and practices that all normalize violence in language and discourse and in practice. When I experienced Charlottesville, it was clear to me that white liberal progressives felt like they had the answer to the Unite the Right audience. But oppositional politics and the ways that our political system maintains a binary in its approach will not heal the wounds of systemic violence. These civic and political norms will not create an embodied life. Nonoppositional politics will, relationships will, embodied difference will!

Civic life requires connection; embodiment requires a felt sense of the materiality of the body. When these two realities conjoin, the potentiality of new contours of becoming emerges. And that emergence can begin to chart a horizon of embodiment. In many ways, this emergence is an unbecoming of becoming that initiates new folds of becoming.

MIND, BODY, SKIN, SCARS

When I was sixteen, my grandfather told me he thought I was crazy.

We were sitting at lunch with my grandmother at a Luby's in Texas. I loved going to Luby's to have chicken-fried steak and cherry pie. My grandfather and I always got the same thing! I had just recovered from two brain surgeries to repair damage from an aneurysm, and to my grandfather, that meant I was crazy. I don't know where he got his logic or how he thought that was a good and helpful thing to tell me, but he didn't hold back.

I had a great neurosurgeon, Dr. David Dean; he saved my life. The aneurysm was the size of a small orange, they tell me, and after being in a coma for three days, I fully recovered. But the medicine I was on messed with my body, fucked up my metabolism. I gained weight at an accelerated speed, and I've still not been able to mitigate the extra weight with diet or exercise. It was the first time my white father told me I was fat. We were shopping for clothes for the end-of-the-year concert, and I asked if I looked fat. I don't know where I learned that question, but beauty standards already were conscripted into my young mind.

Brain surgery changed a lot of things. I became scared to die, I felt (or rather didn't feel at all but knew myself to be) separate from my body, and I learned to live with this new-formed fear.

Later, when I was in my clinical pastoral education training for chaplaincy, my admission of my fear of death created an antagonism between me and my supervisor. He thought that he knew everything, including my own biases and fear of death. He was a Lutheran pastor and one of those old-school guys who had an answer for everything. He believed his antagonism would somehow help me, but all it did was piss me off and remind me that once again, another white man wasn't listening to me when I spoke about my fear of dying. When will we ever begin to practice empathy when people share their fears and concerns with us? And living through a global health pandemic, that fear of death resurfaced in new and strange ways. Even though the disconnection is not material, I can feel and sense the separation between mind and body, the disconnection in my emotional self. I am still becoming. *Poco a poco*, as they say.

My adolescent years were some of the hardest of my life—learning how to live as one who survived a brain aneurysm and also learning to live disconnected from my body. As my brain healed, the medications essential to the healing process also shaped and shifted my body. I internalized ideas that I was unworthy and fat, a narrative reinforced by my father. And it's really fucking hard to become embodied when all you're hearing are negative messages. So many of us live with the scripts that we are unworthy and are failures. I wish we were better at being human with one another.

In and through all of this, I was navigating my own gender identity and imagination around masculinity. I didn't fully embody my body or learn how to body my feelings until much later. I know I was dealing with the trauma of brain surgery and the fear that the bleeding in my brain might happen again. Each time I had some sensation in my head or a headache, I was held captive to my own imagination that I was dying again. My pupils were fixed and dilated once in 1993 just prior to the emergency brain surgery; I was clinically dead. Might it happen again? Was one of the sensations I was having a sign? It's been almost twenty-five years since my brain surgeries, and only recently have I allowed a person to touch my head. We are all so starved for touch in a myriad of ways, and one of the things that I now love is having my head massaged, but for years, I buried that desire. I've just gotten into my body enough to allow anyone—including even my companion, an expert in somatics—to touch the scar.

Being disembodied is a constant struggle to stay grounded in my body. But I know embodiment brings healing. When I release the disembodiment and lean into the radical embodiment of becoming—when I body my becoming and my feelings—I know my mind and body will be free. That is my journey now and will be for the rest of my life. I have not perfected this fold of my becoming.

It's a journey that is intimately related to coming to recognize myself, to being at home in my body. Even though I wake up each morning in a body I don't recognize, I struggle to feel the connection "from head to tail," as they say in somatics class. From the literal head of our bodies to the tail of our spine, there is a connection. Can you feel it?

It has taken me months to feel the connection, but if I move head to tail and rotate both head and tail, I can feel the connection; I can feel my body becoming embodied, and I can sense my materiality as I incorporate movement into the work of embodiment. It almost feels magical to me—that my body is connecting with itself in this new way. I sometimes can't believe it, but I keep trying with the hope of feeling my body. As a person on the autism spectrum, I can't feel my body unless someone is touching me. I wonder how many other people can't feel their bodies due to trauma or neurodivergence. It can be scary not to be able to feel, and it is freeing to be able to feel and body our feelings.

I've never been much of an athlete. In high school, I was into music, and even now I am much more cerebral and artistic than I am sporty. I don't like to sweat unless I have to; in fact, I have some dysphoria around sweating, though the discovery of being on the autism spectrum has actually given me a new language and a new understanding of sensory overload. The sweating isn't dysphoria; it's actually a sensory overload. Getting wet—rain falling, for instance—also causes sensory overload, though I'm able to shower. I haven't quite been able to put my finger on the discomfort of sweating yet; maybe I connect sweat to being overly masculine in a toxic way. And even though I dose testosterone, I'm clear in my body; I'm not trying to be a man. Yet as my body absorbs this new vitamin, my body is more apt to sweat more and smell different. I've even changed deodorants so that I can smell decent and not smell like a man, whatever and however men smell. But this is also a sensory thing my brain needs to accept and like. I like to smell clean because my Mexican mother told me people used to call her dirty when she was growing up. There's a lot to unpack from the stories I was told and the ways I was raised by a Mexican woman who faced racism daily and still does.

What will I do when my body begins to smell because it has a higher level of T in it? I will breathe through the experience and seek to ground my intention in the art and act of becoming embodied. Thinking back to the disparaging remarks my family of origin made after I had brain surgery to repair the aneurysm, I wonder if they knew what a gift my life was. I wonder if they imagined me into adulthood. Could they imagine I would work to restore body and mind? So many of us have families who don't support us or create conditions for our flourishing. I am just one example.

I don't know if they had the imagination to fathom who I was becoming. The two brain surgeries were and are a part of my disembodiment *and* my embodiment. Just like the dosing of T is part of regenerating my becoming embodied. I am *la naguala*, a shape-shifter. It is part of my resistance.

I've written about my mother, who is from Mexico. But she rarely claims that home of origin. She has five birth certificates, all manufactured by others for her. Maybe including those created by some family. She is Brown, visibly Mexican. When she married my father, an Anglo man, and when she gave birth to me, a melanin-deficient and conditionally white baby, she and my father created another birth certificate—mine. Especially now in the war against Black and Brown bodies, embodying whiteness on my skin has been the hardest journey of my life. It is the radical difference I seek to be connected with—the center of my own difference: conditionally white.

Coming across as white passing, lately I've been thinking about my usage of the terms *people of color* and *person of color*. They reify whiteness and make white the norm. I much prefer to use a framework of colorlessness, though I know that is insufficient too. I am a mixed-raced Latinx, yes, and I am white passing, yes, but in this scheme of "race," I am colorless; I am an otherwise being. I like to reframe *white passing* to being "conditionally white." I am conditionally white, which means I'm afforded the benefits of whiteness along with the accompanying suspicion and scrutiny from those who are darker skinned. As a mixed-raced Latinx, my work is to continually undermine supremacy culture in every way. It's in my scholarship, in my behaviors, and in my speaking engagements. This is the work that has called me—that we might become a more perfect union. It takes all of us. My job is to use these privileges to undermine white supremacy and these perils to more deeply investigate what race really is.

I perform whiteness in many ways, and I perform Latinidad in others. I sometimes wonder if I will embody Latinidad in my bones when the norm of whiteness seeps through the pores of my skin. During my doctoral program, I remember researching the concept of porosity and learning that flesh is the most porous organ of our body. Does race seep into the pores of our skin? Does our flesh speak race? Or is race entirely socially constructed, only visible as a concept that organizes bodies?

When I'm in Mexico or anywhere in Latin America, I feel things that I don't normally feel when I'm in the States. Several years ago, for example, when I was in Oaxaca, Mexico, my ancestral home, I literally could feel in my bones the struggle my mother's family had when they migrated north to Texas. Several generations back, my mother's family migrated from Oaxaca and to Nuevo León, the Mexican state just across the border from Texas.

My family fled poverty and injustice in Mexico, and by the time I was born in the mid-1970s, my mother had left her family to find her freedom, migrating into Texas. There my mother helped me assimilate into whiteness. I was five before I realized we were a different shade.

She was Brown; I was . . . white? White? Was I white, or was I colorless?

I was born to a Mexican immigrant and Anglo man in the piney woods of Longview, Texas, in 1976. I came to know the word *difference* at an early age, and this has propelled me into the work that I do now—helping steward connection with difference, with the center of my own difference, and with the difference of others.

I couldn't have predicted that my encounter with the concept of difference would create a whole orientation around my studies and scholarship. Knowledge *does* create power, as the Black Panthers taught.

When my dark, caramelly Brown mother asked me if anyone ever made fun of the color of my skin, I discovered difference. In her asking me that question, for the first time, I realized that she was not like me—or was it that I was not like her?

My mother always made sure I understood that everyone should be treated with kindness and compassion. I was now recognizing myself as different, and it didn't occur to me that this would mean the world might treat me differently because of how I was taught to treat people and how I was taught to expect to be treated.

At the time, *race* was not a part of my vocabulary, but when I moved to live with my white father in San Antonio, Texas, my father pushed me to check the box "Hispanic" to receive college funding. Another moment of realizing that I was different. Now that I was old enough to realize that "different" also meant that you could receive college funding, I was curious. At this point, I was a high school senior and had an awareness of bodied difference (Black, white, Asian, Mexican), but I didn't quite have the awareness that these differences were actually situated within a socially constructed system called *race*. I had heard the term *racism* and had even witnessed my white father and white grandfather using the N-word to describe Black people, and when I would ask my father not to use that word, I was met with a deafening silence. This was also my experience; this is how I entered my own sensibilities concerning difference.

What transpired as I grew into adulthood was this awareness of being different but not knowing where I belonged. I didn't feel comfortable marking "white" on forms when I had this embodied awareness of being different. I knew my mother was Brown and Mexican and my father was white, but I didn't know how to situate myself in a conversation about race, nor did that language ever come up for me until I was in college. Even then I was surrounded by a whole host of white folks, so conversations around race did not happen for me until I moved to Chicago.

Because of my skin color, I learned how to negotiate spaces of power and privilege but didn't associate that negotiation with race until much later, when I would come to realize that this is how race often works: there are mechanisms in place that help people with skin color like mine and mechanisms in place that hurt people with skin color that is darker than mine. It's always both/and, and this awareness is what compels me to be wise as a serpent.

At the age of five years old, the only meaning I assigned to the question my mother asked me—"Does anyone ever make fun of you for the color of your skin?"—was that I was different. Difference, then, became an animating technology for me, one that I embraced and one that I needed to embody so that I could make meaning of my raced body. I have been in a process of an unbecoming becoming as I metabolize the gravity of the difference I embody and the awareness that continues to accelerate within me.

Now as an adult, I move in the world with power, access, and privilege because I've had access to college and higher education, which came because I left living with my mother in 1989 and went to live with my white father. That is where I learned both Latinidad and whiteness. I learned how to code switch. I learned how to navigate things culturally. But my body was still read as white, conditionally speaking.

I spent my summers in Monterrey, Mexico. I loved being in Mexico. I still love making frequent trips to my ancestral home in Oaxaca, where the food is amazing and the people are so very warm! I stay with the same family each time I return "home." One summer when I was living with my white father, we had a family reunion in Cozumel, Mexico, where one of my aunts owned a hotel. I had a room to myself and from the room's window could see the ocean crashing against the hotel. I even got to scuba dive on that trip. This was before the brain surgery. I got to enjoy Mexico with family. I got to speak Spanish and eat amazing food. I felt this in my body. I didn't know it at the time, but those were moments of embodiment.

Even a sense of family, of location, of belonging—at least for summers—in a culture, though, didn't exactly solve the problem of my skin color being white or white passing or even colorless. What do mixed-raced folks do when they fall between categories? How do we embody our culture and our race? What is our culture and what is our race?

We are those folks who are betwixt, and therefore our embodiment will be in that liminal space of becoming. Perhaps that is my goal in the work of embodiment. Perhaps that is what I need to be paying attention to—to the *work of becoming*—instead of striving so hard for a *feeling of embodiment*. Feelings are elusive, after all. But the work of embodiment is the striving to be deeply embodied.

It's not redundant to consider embodiment the work to be working to embody. It is hard work, especially for those of us who are light-skinned or fall in between categories.

What is the embodiment that we are to embody? Is there such a thing as a mixed embodiment?

How do we breathe that kind of embodiment into existence?

Lately, I've been reading a lot of articles on weight, weight loss, and nutrition. I've been thinking about my body and how I need to be healthier; I've been thinking how Big Pharma in the form of a little pill caused me to gain weight at an accelerated speed and have health markers that were death-bringing. So I've committed to being on a journey to care for my body in radical ways that help not only bring my health markers to a better place but also cultivate a body that can sustainably do this work of embodiment.

I've recently discovered how trauma shows up in me as I read about bodies considered fat or overweight—imprinting trauma. There are stories I've imprinted about bodies, and pain and grief are a part of that imprint.

Our brains are magical machines. They hold so much information. I am curious to learn how to shift and metabolize the traumatic memories into ones that help me flourish and help others with their journeys around their bodies. Our bodies are not mechanical devices; we are fluid and embodied, and everything is in motion. But here in the West, much of our embodiment has been stolen from us because we live in a Cartesian worldview. Along with Descartes, we privilege the mind, and so we move in the world from the shoulders up. That's one of the things I'm trying to shift as I read about weight, food, and nutrition. How do I move from an embodied place, and how do I live from an embodied place? How do we shift that standpoint to where it is alive and buoyed by embodiment?

It might seem strange to bring up nutrition as part of the work of embodiment, but when we have a relationship with the food we are eating, we become more aligned with the energetic folds of creation. Plants and animals all have energy, and when we learn to be in communion with this energy, we become closer to having an orientation around embodiment when it comes to our food. Of course, we aren't taught this in society. We are taught that food and eating are transactions in which we participate, but what happens when we think of food and nutrition as part of the whole-body relationship we are trying to have?

This past year, while the first fold of the pandemic was surging, my partner and I decided to join a community-supported agriculture (CSA) program that connected us with a woman-owned organic farm. We did this to reduce our dependency on grocery store shopping and invest in small farms feeding our community. Living in Tennessee, there are lots of farms, and thankfully, these farmers grow food to feed their communities.

Among the community farms is Bloomsbury Farm in Smyrna. We drive out to the farm each Friday to pick up our veggies, and we go to the farm because we like to see what all the options are. This way, I feel as though I have a relationship with the food and the land from which it comes, and the farmers are also in relationship with the land, the crops, and the community. One great thing about the farm is that Lauren, the farmer, hands out beer as we all wait in line for our turn to get our veggies. So I get to enjoy some craft beer on a farm and enjoy all the sights as we wait. There are so many different animals on the farm, from dogs and cats to goats and ducks. It's amazing to see all of this created life each Friday! This has changed the ways I feel about how my body absorbs the energy that I am digesting. Another shift that we have made is buying from a local butcher shop. For my body to feel grounded and embodied, I need more protein than the average person. So Bare Bones Butcher here in Nashville, Tennessee, has been our go-to place for fresh chicken, ground beef, sausage, and lamb. I get that this sounds like privilege around food and access. I'd agree: the ability to take time, to drive, to choose, to connect to the land when so many of us don't feel we have resources beyond a chain big-savings grocery store and a slim paycheck. After all, I am also living paycheck to paycheck! What I've discovered in my body is related not only to food sources but to fair pay for labor; when those who work in the fields are fairly paid, those who serve the local community are supported. Embodiment is both personal and social; it is highly relational, and not only do I sense the relationship between the food I am eating; I feel that sense of connection in my body, my emotional well-being feels more stable and grounded, as I am delighted in consuming in a way that feels relational, supports relationship, and in many ways is a new vision for social democracy.

I was given so many lessons about difference and my body from my family, lessons that were trauma in my body. As I understand, unlearn, unembody to embody, I am learning to body my feelings and my food. It does take a village!

Embodiment reorients our whole selves into a better-aligned relationship with all we encounter every day. Embodiment isn't a transaction; it is finding yourself in the deepest parts of who you are and living from that place.

IV
REPETITION

Repetition relates to connection. Repetition contrasts generality. While generality often refers to events connected through cycles, equalities, and laws, it doesn't refer to specific circumstances or relations of connection. Most phenomena recorded and attributed to science or described by science are presented in generalities; to my mind, this is not repetition but more like summary. And isolated events will occur over and over because they are governed or stabilized by these same laws. In the circumstance of water, we know that it will flow downhill because it is governed by gravity. As my partner—who is a dancer and choreographer—sometimes says when something falls unexpectedly, "Gravity is a bitch." Likewise, sunlight will create warmth because of principles that apply broadly. We also know that due to the science of climate change, the earth will continue to become warmer. In the human realm, behaviors that accord with norms and laws count as generalities for similar reasons. Science deals mostly with generalities because it seeks to predict reality using reduction and equivalence.

Repetition is important here because it allows for difference to emerge. When we move away from generalities and into the terrain of difference, we get to imagine what is possible. Difference and repetition always go together for me.

THE HEALING POWER
OF SOMATICS

Dismantling supremacy culture is work I began to envision after being in Charlottesville in 2017. I have now come to understand that the work of dismantling something, while intended to be positive, frames it within a negative, so I now use the language of *compost*, drawing from my studies in ecology and ecotheology and animal studies. This word feels more active and generative than *dismantle* and doesn't carry the negative energy that *dismantle* tends to embody.

I now work to *compost supremacy culture*, which requires an embodied awareness to be in relationship with what is and what is hoped for. This wisdom comes in and through the work of somatics, which in part helps me engage questions like *What kind of body do you want to have to help steward the work of equity and justice?*—a question not about ability but about awareness of relationship with one's body that can chart wisdom for the kind of work needed to change our culture.

In the fall of 2018, I led a workshop called "Dismantling Supremacy Culture," sponsored by the organization Imaginarium. At the end of the workshop, a beautiful human approached me and asked me if I ever thought of incorporating the body into my work.

A year before this fateful meeting, I was in rural Connecticut at a Jewish retreat center and was introduced to the field of somatics. I considered my own work as a theologian, ethicist, and activist and knew that my first book, *Activist Theology*, was more than a thinking project, yet it was missing the body. And so I began a journey of coming to understand somatics and sought to find connections to help me learn more and incorporate this modality into my work and teaching.

Up until the time of the workshop, I'd been unsuccessful in finding a sustainable connection with anyone who might help me incorporate somatics into the Activist Theology Project (ATP). But the question following that workshop helped open the possibilities for somatics to steward me in my work as a public theologian and in my body, since I was already on a journey to(ward) embodiment. I see now how that meeting and my leaning into somatics have shifted my work as a public theologian to being a politicized theologian, privileging the body as the primary site for transforming culture.

That fateful meeting turned into a collaboration that continues to this day. I am so grateful for the relationship that I share with Erin C. Law. She is not only my beloved partner; she is also my somatics educator and collaborator in the work at ATP. Soon after we met, Erin joined the team at ATP, bringing an art to facilitation and an embodied wisdom that has deepened the work in important ways.

Somatics is a slow, functional movement. It is not designed to be exercise, though some movements might feel like exercise. Somatics invites us into the art of feeling our materiality, sensing our materiality, and experiencing our materiality—a real piece of connection with body and mind. Not long after we started dating, I began attending Erin's somatics class in Nashville. I wanted to incorporate this kind of movement into the work I was creating and attempting to imagine. On a gut level, I knew social healing was more than information, more than learning statistics, more than saying, "Black lives matter." But I didn't have a felt sense of the work in my body—something I sensed I desperately needed.

So each Thursday, I attended Erin's somatics class. Many who came to the class were much older than me; they were keeping themselves moving and limber. I was deeply humbled to be in class with these individuals and to learn from them as they shared their own experiences with their bodies and somatics.

As someone who grew up with a Mexican mother who told me to never get dirty, lying on the floor became a learning experience that replaced voices of fear and anxiety for me. I learned how to put my body in relationship with gravity, with the floor, with what is grounding us all in this life, a powerful lesson as I continue to work to ground myself in a felt sense of my materiality.

When the pandemic grew into a global concern, Erin facilitated their class over Zoom. The class grew as people from all over the country joined. And I focused on small, functional movements to help me cope and deal with living in a pandemic. As many in 2020 did, we created a small community together on Zoom. And we grounded our community in the work of somatics. On one occasion and related to the class, Erin invited me to lie on her massage table, and she offered some touch through the modality of bodywork (she's also a licensed massage therapist). I was invited to reflect and write on how I experienced the touch and how my body felt.

Knowing my desire to deepen my awareness of the felt sense of my body, Erin invited me to bring reflection, to give language to what I'm feeling and what I am sensing. This work is important not only to my body but to the democratic body, important for the larger work of social healing I wish to facilitate.

I wrote about the experience, both in anticipation of the work and after the session, and these are among my reflections:

PRESESSION

Erin asked me to reflect on this question: What are three things I notice in my body right now using feeling or sensation language?

I feel open—openness is something that I long to achieve. Open to my body, open to the sensations that my body yields. I've been closed off from my own self for so many years due to fatigue, trauma, and other harm-related incidents.

I feel calm—I sense and know that I am in a trusted environment, so I feel calm. I feel cared for, and I feel held. So much of my restlessness came from not being in a trusted environment where I could be my complete self, and now I am my full self, complete in my becoming bodied.

I feel satisfied—I've just eaten lunch, so I feel both satisfied and satiated. As I sip on my kombucha from Folklore Ferments, I experience the satisfaction of feeling grounded in my body. There's a certain satisfaction to that feeling that I'm discovering in these moments.

POSTSESSION

Following the massage, Erin asked me this question and asked me to reflect on it: What are three things I notice in my body right now using feeling or sensation language?

I feel a deep relaxation in my body-soul.

I am knit together, like I am intended to be.

I am being held with sacred awareness for my healing.

My head feels whole and complete.

I could feel the connection between my kidney and leg; I imagine my kidney present protecting me.

I feel like all the hatches are opening for me to explore myself.

I have often offered this reflection when sharing my journey around bodily healing through somatics. It's useful to record aspects of a journey toward healing, and among the various interventions, somatics has afforded me tools to deepen my relationship with my journey of embodiment, enlivening my thinking through listening to my *soma*, my feeling body.

Embodiment requires we listen to the *soma*, to what is alive in us. Our bodies are alive, and if we further a felt sense of our bodies and practice connection with and to our bodies, we foster somatic awareness—a connective practice that our culture does not support. Our world facilitates transactions and exchanges unbuoyed by a somatic awareness, and the reigning connection is grounded in the mechanics of thinking and doing, not becoming, not embodied.

This missing piece in our culture is causing us as a society to not be in our *somas* and therefore to have a chaotic and discombobulated cultural *soma*. Creating life-affirming systems requires being embodied, which is why I've turned to the work of *somatic abolition*, a phrase I borrow from Resmaa Menakem. Menakem, a trauma-informed therapist and facilitator, uses somatics as a way to intervene in our social justice world. When we steward a sustainable relationship with our *soma*, we can begin to steward a culture that is responsible and responsive to the contours of embodiment. This is the ground of somatic abolition and also the work of our collaborative project: Activist Theology Project. When we imagine a better world, may we imagine connections with the felt sense of our bodies.

"I change myself; I change the world." Years ago, when I was in seminary, I read these words from Gloria Anzaldúa, words that seem so somatically informed. The work of somatics not only changes us but can ultimately change the world, and what Gloria Anzaldúa did in her writing, throughout her art and poetry, and in her coalitional organizing is to shape and shift the inner landscape of herself and others so that our world can become the change we so desperately need and want. Since reading those words all those years ago, I still believe their truth: if we can shift the work of justice and equity to be grounded in embodied work and relationship work, we might be able to build the kind of world we long to inhabit.

This quote from Anzaldúa speaks to somatics, which requires a relationship with body and mind, and when that connection is made, through the ways we shift how we are with ourselves, we, in connection with others, shift those relationships as well. Not that the mind and body are an assumed disconnection but that there is a cultural disconnection of our bodies that accelerates disconnection within our cultural body.

The relational framework of somatics creates conditions for a culture shift. There are many people who can't or

won't engage in the work of somatics. Even our social justice industrial complex is often disembodied from the work
those in justice intend to steward. If disembodiment is created by the mechanics, and there is no relational grounding
to the work, what I've experienced is a kind of competitive-
ness that often mimics the dominant culture—the very
culture that the social justice industrial complex is seeking
to shift.

To steward relationship and connection in the work we
are doing in the world, we have to remember that relationship with self and body is what enables us to support connection and relationship with others. When we imagine the
kind of connection that sustains equity and justice, we can
then begin to practice our work in the vein of somatic abolition, done in community.

As I was preparing to launch the work of ATP, I knew my
work was more than intellectual labor and more than what
can emerge from the mind; it also demanded the body.
Realizing that I had been on a journey to bridge together
body and mind (and develop a relationship with my body),
somatics taught me to feel different parts of my body from
the inside out. Somatics class was humbling; I learned not
only to root my body to the gravitational pull of the ground
but then to get up off the ground, to rise up (something I
was chided for as a child due to internalized oppression
my Mexican biological mother held within her body).
During the early days of quarantine, I would join the Sunday somatics class with people from all over the country

seeking to compost the anxiety and fear of a raging virus by slowing down, getting into our bodies, and practicing a relationship with our bodies. These were also practices of cultivating awareness, intentionally slowing down and rooting ourselves in our bodies, and listening. The work of healing requires we listen to our bodies and learn from cellular wisdom.

Several years ago, everyone was talking about Bessel van der Kolk's book *The Body Keeps the Score*. And it was among the reasons I turned to somatics. If the body does, indeed, keep the score, how do we create a sustainable relationship with what the body internalizes, and what do we need to compost to be free? It's a question I continue to ask in imagining the soma to its fullest expression.

We still live in a world that dominates a moral and religious framework, failing to encourage the body to be a piece of the puzzle to being a full self. As a theologian and ethicist, I want to challenge that and push our culture, including our religious and moral traditions, to see the body as an important catalyst for a culture shift. Among the best tools we have to compost supremacy culture and steward a cultural body into thriving by embracing our resiliency is somatics.

Somatics work is also related to democracy. When we support connection with all the different but interrelated and interconnected parts of ourselves, we are stewarding a practice of generous connection with others. Practicing generous self-humanity, we shift our interpersonal relationships. Somatics is an individual endeavor; it is the practice of supporting a healthier cultural body, which in turn helps steward the kind of world we long to inhabit. What kind of humans do we want to be? Again, I return to the question I've been asking since I was in Charlottesville.

THE POLITICS OF BODIES IN MOTION

Our world is composed of motion. The global movement of bodies has created a postnationalist world. Borders precede states and sovereignty, and in fact, it is the global movement of bodies that creates and re-creates borders, which then create and re-create states.

There is a politics to bodies in motion, and as I've reflected on my own life of movement and nomadism—a preferred orientation to help further destabilize any sort of stasis of place—I have come to see the importance of not only analyzing bodies in motion but seeing this politicized motion as a way to reimagine our world and quite possibly influence visions for a more just democracy.

Earlier this year, I watched the Netflix series *Move*. This series showed the power and influence of movement and dance. The first episode showed how street dance became an important modality in shaping dance studios in Los

Angeles. The episode followed two young men—a Black man from Memphis and a man of color from Miami—who converged in LA, tirelessly working their way up in different studios that might create conditions for them to have their own dance company. Eventually, they began collaborating and helping young people through dance education, which in turn shaped various communities. Dance does have the power to shape whole communities, as *Move* narrates, but often, dance is undervalued, and many times, artists are expected to work for free. Another episode followed a young woman in Jamaica who reframes dancehall—a historically male-dominated form of dance—through a feminist lens. Now dancehall is being revolutionized by leading women. Movement is reshaping communities!

Move helps me see the global movement of bodies in relationship. Movement dominates our entertainment and political landscapes, yet those who harness movement as an important modality are able to reshape our imagination for a better world.

Yes, many say that art will heal our wounds and save us, and I believe that too, but often that belief fails to take into account the ways in which motion is the primary way that culture is made and remade. This is where the politics of bodies in motion can truly revolutionize our awareness and our practices in making culture.

At present, we have a cultural system that exploits people, especially those on the underside, and extracts from these communities in order to preserve an artificial resilience and cultural supremacy that accelerates whiteness and the toxicities of whiteness. Because we don't have a humane system for those moving in and through our country, we have encouraged a cultural approach to the global movement of bodies through the criminalization of migrants, the exploitation of their labor, and their ongoing extraction. We have culturally created a funnel system that not only accelerates this exploitation and extraction but also financially incentivizes private institutions to quell the movement and ultimately extract these bodies from our country. Why is this important to a book on becoming embodied? Because if we don't learn to steward the global movement of bodies in a way that creates conditions for livability for all, especially those on the underside, we will not be able to steward democracy in embodied ways. Our culture will be gravely compromised by our greed and consumption of migrant labor, and we will fail to be the kind of humanity that is generous with one another.

In the global movement of bodies, the primacy of motion is important to reshaping our relationship with bodies in motion. In our current reality, we have a criminalized transactional relationality with bodies in motion and bodies crossing borders. But how can you cross a border that is always moving? Humans have made up these borders and placed them superficially on top of what is actually a seamless and interconnected planetary body. The punishment doesn't make sense, because the body of the earth itself is in constant motion. This is a global concern, not just a concern for the United States. And because we don't know how to care for the other as a culture, we end up accelerating patterns of cultural trauma with migrants in ways that expand societal harm.

We are all conscripted into supremacy culture, even these bodies who seemingly move freely across borders. Their imagined freedom is eviscerated by the cultural trauma that has gone unprocessed for centuries, and they and we are caught up in a cycle of repetition of harm that creates and re-creates our state of being and becoming.

What was so powerful about *Move* was the show's ability to capture not only the imagination of movement but also the power of the courage to use movement as a form of personal and social healing. Movement can truly be both revolutionary and transformative! When we can take steps to use movement in more imaginative and healing ways, we can reshape and reimagine the global movement of bodies and the impact this kind of movement has on our society. When we are able to do this kind of imaginative work, we can also begin to reshape our norms and values as a culture with hopes of healing the cultural trauma that has long instituted norms and values that contribute to the unprecedented societal harm carried through generations.

Motion is one of the most primitive ideas we have. And we have used this idea of motion to harm countless people, thus creating a culture that devalues those of us who move around, about, through, and across. I remember my own journeys and migratory patterns. These were necessary for me to continue with my training in graduate school. I was constantly in motion, and yet the critique I received of that movement was that I needed to stop moving and settle down in one place. Why? Movement destabilizes things, places, and people, and if we can move in just and equitable ways, we can reshape our democracy.

A lot of people think in terms of "settling," and it's probably why we, as a culture, have a one-dimensional perspective on life that doesn't value—doesn't have—a relationship to space and place. Before I left my faculty post in Berkeley, California, and moved home to the South, I used my nomadism as a way to destabilize this one-dimensional perspective on life.

I wanted to be in relationship with all of our culture, not just the few square miles I lived and inhabited. I felt my orientation to nomadism was a kind of deterritorialism that created conditions for me to shift my relationship with space and place and offered me an opportunity to deepen my awareness of the mechanisms of our democratic society here in the United States.

Instead of choosing one place to make my home, I chose movement over stasis and had several homes, but this came out of a necessity for community. I found a home with people, and these people helped me reimagine my relationship with space and place. This has been an important journey in discovering who I am in the world and how I have a body in this world. Of course, much of my nomadism came during a time when I was completing graduate school. I didn't feel connected to any space and place in Chicago during seminary or in Colorado when I was working on my PhD. Following my doctoral program, I sought to be in relationship with other Queer-identified folks who lived in various places in the United States. When I would travel to speak at churches, community centers, or colleges and universities, I would stay with my friends. This nomadic life taught me how important having a relationship to space and place is and how my need to be embodied also included the need for me to ground myself in space and place.

Though my family has had to migrate from one country, how might I envision a life that is fully connected to all that is? Nomadism, inspired by two of my favorite philosophers, Gilles Deleuze and Rosi Braidotti, helped me imagine how movement could deterritorialize space and place. Nomadism might be able to infuse difference and multiplicity into a space and place that had been colonized by white-bodied folks and others who used power, access, and privilege to disconnect and displace the native people. I didn't own property, so my version of "multiple homes" was sharing living spaces with people who I considered to be chosen family, and I found that my movement across this country and my opportunities to spend time in multiple places not only shaped my life but also shaped my awareness of the fact that our democracy is not stabilized as a thing in itself; our democracy is dynamic because of the movement that is present in our culture.

Motion is also a way that we can imagine building the necessary bridges to be with people who are different from us. Movement between cultures and people groups creates conditions for connection and new folds of relationalities to emerge in an otherwise static and stable imagination of the state of things. I think about my own movement relative to my gender identity. My "transition" as a NonBinary Transgender Latinx has been a kind of destabilizing what I know about myself and a deterritorializing of the norms and values that are assigned to bodies of difference. The relationship that I have created with my body has been one of movement, both internally and externally. The foundation of that relationship has been movement.

And the politics of that movement are found embedded in my bodily practices, from where I buy coffee to where I buy my needles for my T shots. What I am trying to illustrate is that our most difficult policies in this country that impact us as a culture are also practices that stem from our bodies. Our politics and policies are not disconnected from our bodies or our social practices, however much we try to privilege disembodied politics. Our politics and policies in this country impact real bodies, and many of these bodies are disenfranchised and have performed enormous amounts of movement to cross treacherous terrain to arrive in a country that only exploits them and then extracts them from their culture. Movement is at the heart of everything we do in this culture. Who can move and who is forbidden? I think it's important to hold this complex question so that we can create movements that are not forced or harmful for those who are participating in globalized motion. And if we don't begin to have a better relationship with both motion and our politics, we will continue to accelerate cultural harm through politics and policies that target those who do move in and out of our culture.

I moved to Nashville in 2017 and was unable to get a driver's license until I had a utility bill in my name. My car was registered to a family address in Arkansas. My entire life has been marked by movement in many respects, and when I decided to create space and place in Nashville for my work and life, the system currently in place wouldn't allow me to be a part of the Tennessee community until I had proof that I was not mobile. I am not the only victim of this; people without homes aren't able to get jobs because they don't have permanent addresses. Though unhoused people are living on land, which is in constant movement, they don't have the same privileges as those who are able to collect their mail from a mailbox. Employers won't give people who don't have permanent addresses a chance. These are the real victims of the criminalization of movement and mobility, yet this kind of movement is often due to natural disaster, poverty, war, and countless other things.

We not only criminalize migrants for their movement across borders; we also punish others who move about in nomadic ways. From a policy and political level, we discourage movement. What this also does is create a culture that internalizes a belief that we should not be moving. When we create a culture that does not move, we also create the conditions for a disembodied culture, separated from motion in profound ways and accelerating violence from both establishment and community.

What results from this disembodied culture is what we see today—the rise of white nationalism from within our government and the communities that support this rise in our established government. We can't get away from any of what is happening. It's the water in which we are swimming. Motion and movement are staples among us; they help destabilize and deterritorialize the stasis of supremacy culture that creates manifold harm.

The question I have is, *How do we hold motion and stability together as a both/and component for a healthy, vibrant multivocal democracy?* What we need for conditions of possibility to create a multivocal movement of a participatory democracy are movement and the global reality of motion within this world. It's the stasis of supremacy culture that we are seeking to compost because there is stability in mobility that often makes a kind of figure eight around us all. We traverse this figure eight of mobility and stability, and each time we land on a different spot, we are able to cast a different, more robust vision.

What we so desperately need is the embodied solidarity of a multivocal participatory democracy. Motion and mobility help facilitate some of that, but we also need to be able to create lasting relationships with place. I think about the native communities who stewarded the land that is now called Nashville, Tennessee. This land has been cared for by Cherokee, Yuchi, and Shawnee peoples, and because of the way settler colonialism works, we've all macerated the existing relationships with the land and created a transactional relationality with land, people, animals, and the rest of the world.

We need to destabilize the settler mentality so that we can shape and shift our current vision of democracy into one of multiplicity and difference. Motion and movement help us do that, and we carry those folds within us each and every day. We just need to pay attention to what's bubbling up within us and what the felt sense is of what we are hoping to create, continually asking, What kind of world do we long to inhabit?

EMBODIMENT AS A VISION FOR DEMOCRACY

I have long thought that there is a connection between our lived experience and the ways we create policies in our cities and in our nation's capital. But it wasn't until I began to consider the body and our relationship with our bodies that I began to think in a much larger way about our culture and evolving democracy.

On January 6, 2021, in Washington, DC, a large number of white nationalists and white supremacists sought to take over the US Capitol. Many of these men and women were armed, donning fatigues as well as Christian symbols.

As I watched the MSNBC broadcast of what was transpiring, I couldn't help but see very clearly the merging of white Christian supremacy with white-bodied supremacy. Many people have called what transpired an attempted coup to overthrow the election and prevent Joe Biden from being inaugurated as the next president.

There was an acceleration of the governing arm of white militias to subvert the democratic process and sow seeds of fascism, and the attempts at a coup or other subversions of the democratic process and the new presidency continued. Just weeks before the inauguration of Joe Biden, security and surveillance accelerated, and the hum of additional attempts to overtake state capitols or the US Capitol continued. Given how deeply polarized we are in this historical moment, I've always known this is possible.

I mention the events that many of us witnessed on news media and via social media because it raises a larger issue of the state of our wellness as a cultural body. What transpired on January 6, 2021, is also the result of unprocessed trauma living in bodies and accelerated by white-bodied supremacy to the point that people sought to overtake the US Capitol. I also realize that this country has been occupied by white-bodied supremacy and the agenda of white supremacy, whose infrastructure has been anti-Blackness, anti-Semitism, and anti-Difference since its inception.

The trauma of our democracy has fueled a cultural body that foments violence and accelerates polarization. We are not just traumatized by our reality; we are also a disembodied cultural body. Knowing this, what does it mean to steward connection with our own bodies so we can then steward connection to our cultural body, which can then shape and shift democracy into a vision for a multiracial, robust participatory democracy that creates conditions for the livability for all, not just the elite?

Because we are so traumatized, we are far from conditions of livability for all as we continue to steward unprocessed trauma as a way of dealing with our issues. Even Congress and the Senate went back into their meetings to certify the 2020 election after the US Capitol was breached by countless men and women. "The show must go on" was the theme. How can our representatives steward democracy when they themselves were obviously victims of the show of white supremacy? There is an urgency to what is procedural, but even our representatives were conscripted into this traumatized cultural body that in turn disconnected and disembodied itself from a democratic vision.

Embodiment is a way forward and to(ward) a kind of democracy that creates conditions for the least of these. But supporting and sustaining this kind of democracy takes so much work both from individuals and from us collectively. In our current culture—a death culture—no environment is provided for to shore up healthy connections, embodied alive connections. Take the way we have all responded to Covid. Take the ways conspiracy theories have accelerated not just white-bodied supremacy but a supremacist state. We have each grown into the conditioning that keeps us apart, that accelerates polarization, and that fuels oppositional politics. There are no conditions for livability under these conditions; they are constraints of supremacy culture.

If we want to transform our culture, we need to consider investing in our own transformation, stewarding practices of embodiment within ourselves so that we can steward an embodied environment within our cultural body.

We use the term *democracy* as if we all agree on what it means. But what do we mean, as a cultural body, by *democracy*? I ask this because as I watch the news and social media, I hear the same terms, but the ways in which these terms get mobilized and played out in policy and government seem very different. So what is democracy and how can democracy in the context of the United States accelerate emancipatory politics and mobilize the project of human freedom and social relations? I ask this question because we cannot think about human freedom or social relations or emancipatory politics outside of relationship with and alongside the body and becoming bodied in ourselves and one another.

Historically, democracy has implied a kind of communalism. Yet what we have inherited in this country is a democracy that continues to depend on hierarchies that accelerate harm. I was talking recently with one of my partner's best friends, a therapist. She described to me the difference between hurt and harm. Hurt can be repaired and is not grounded in intention, whereas harm is intentional and often cannot be repaired.

The democracy we have inherited is harming the least of these, leaving us with the manifold struggle to even imagine what community is. We have all endured a global health pandemic—and continue to do so, even after vaccines have rolled out. And while a lot of white people woke up to the systemic abuse against Black folks when Breonna Taylor was assassinated by the state and when George Floyd was murdered by the state, the work is much more than the act of waking up. Yet in the waking up of white folks, there still were central questions around how to be a community. Comments on Instagram and Twitter called out the performativity of white folks. And as I have stewarded my work in the public square, I have found that a lot of folks just don't know and aren't aware of what is transpiring during this global health pandemic and the rise of what is now known as anti-Black racism. Many are finding themselves in a place of harming the least of these, the underside of history, because they just don't know. We don't know what we don't know, and what we don't know might be the culprit of manifold harm.

Among the most helpful things I learned about racism was that not only is it a social construct leveraged against darker-skinned bodies in the creation of hierarchies; this violence against Black, Brown, Indigenous, and other people of color stems from white-on-white violence originating in England.

As I do each time I give a talk or a lecture or even teach a class, I remind my audience that ideas come from somewhere. And we need to think and ask critically, *From where does violence against darker-skinned bodies come? And how does this kind of violence actually fortify the kind of democracy that we have inherited?* These things are connected, and the violence of supremacy culture has been engineered into the cellular structure and DNA of our society—engineered into our cultural body.

That is why I believe we need to rethink things like motion and democracy. Because when we have a better relationship with the movement of our own bodies, we can calibrate to be in relationship with the movement of other bodies, and this movement helps build an infrastructure of embodiment. And when we can learn to be embodied as individuals, we also learn to have embodied relationships that help reshape our cultural body. This work has the potential to reshape not just our cultural body but our vision for democracy. We *can* imagine another possible world, and we can do this visioning practice *en conjunto*.

This work actually mobilizes and operationalizes the term *participatory* relative to democracy. No longer is democracy a stale word pointing toward the inaction of a government; it is actually mobilizing people to participate in a cultural body and to body their feelings in ways that get shit done. Embodiment is a vision for democracy and requires a diversity of tactics. We all need to not only acknowledge but reckon with how deeply embedded these hegemonic systems are within each of us. When we actually nurture a cultural body that makes a profound break with the dominant system, we can then begin to participate in the stewardship of the logic of liberation. This is why I tell people I am neither conservative nor liberal, neither progressive nor traditional; I am a liberationist and am invested in the logic of liberation.

As I think about the work of healing our democracy, what often feels so overwhelming comes from our focus on one part of that healing process, such as the focus on electoral politics, but when I am thinking about reimagining democracy through a robust lens of participation, I consider that what needs to be healed are the bodies that make up this specific democracy. Healing on a collective scale is what we need in order to put democracy in motion in ways that can help us shape and shift our cultural body.

So much of what is happening right now is the dominant culture (white-bodied folks) reading all the books on how to be antiracist because of the ways that white-bodied folks have been socialized into the banking method. If we bank enough information, then we can be different. In reality, what we need are relationships so that we can shape and shift our reality. And while reading is important, what is needed is an embodied awareness of the impacts of things like racism, militarism, classism, and economic supremacy. White-bodied folks have been socialized in such a way that limits their capacity to learn, glorifying the overintellectualizing and rationalizing of ideas. This is why white-bodied folks often have the talking points around race and racism but don't have an embodied awareness of this work. I see this time and time again, and it's why I have committed to doing relational work in the face of oppositional politics.

Healing our democracy is not neutral work; it is also not limited to just dates, ideas, thoughts, votes, or information. Healing our democracy is part of healing on a collective scale. So participating in a vision for democracy is the ancient practice of world building. When we dream the world we want to inhabit, we can begin to intentionally make it so.

Growing up, I recall hearing the oft-cited "Where there is no vision, people perish," a passage that comes from the Hebrew Bible's book of Proverbs 29:18. How might spending time thinking through and embodying this specific verse help connect the dots to what I have been advocating throughout this book? If I recall my Hebrew Bible training correctly, the entirety of the Hebrew Bible casts a narrative for Israel and the Hebrew people. While the Proverbs verse might be taken as a truism, we could also tie it to this larger vision the writers of the Hebrew Bible attempted to communicate. And what I mean by this is that while many of the books of the Hebrew Bible, specifically, were an elaboration of laws and functions, they were also stories of how communities have been shaped. In these stories, we might see a narrative arc pointing toward a collective vision to be embodied by the Hebrew people or perhaps a vision that we might say comes from God or the Divine, or we might say that the shared relationship between the people who constitute the varying communities of the Hebrew Bible and the Divine helps articulate a vision that accelerates a participatory worldview. Whatever it is, it is about relationship and embodying relationship. We have work to do to get to this point.

There is something prophetic about this vision in the Proverbs verse and in the work of the Hebrew prophets, and there is something to the ways that prophecy calls communities into action and beyond mythic power structures. As I read it again, I wonder if we can look to this passage and lean into a logic of loving liberation that creates conditions for a robust, participatory, multivocal democracy. In the prophetic vision of a logic of loving liberation, might a new world be possible? Might healing on a collective scale emerge? Might there be conditions that we don't yet see because of our wounds and pain and the ways that many of us are just trying to read and consume everything, so we end up missing the mark of having an embodied awareness of the pain and suffering and the need for healing on a collective scale?

Connecting bodies to other bodies helps make up a larger body, which I call our cultural body. And when we have a felt sense of our own bodies, we can be in relationship not only with ourselves but with one another. When this level of relationality is achieved, we can begin to make necessary shifts within our cultural body that accelerate a vision for a different kind of democracy—a kind of possible world that is infused with radical political difference and multiplicity. We can do hard things like imagine the kind of world we want to inhabit. This is the prophetic work of being and becoming embodied. This is what creates conditions for liberation on a collective scale. Embodiment is fundamentally relational. And so is democracy. So when we formulate this equation with attention and attunement toward the logic of liberation, we uncover new paths for collective healing and the work of liberation on a collective scale. Embodiment becomes the primary lens for this pro-phetic vision of a new fold of democracy becoming our re-ality in these critical moments.

The machinations of white-bodied supremacy cultures—seen in the varying pillars of empire, like capitalism and militarism, racism and fascistic politics—point to an over-whelming reality of not only disembodiment but dissocia-tion. I have learned in therapy and from many therapists about the relationship between racialized whiteness and dissociation. When we begin to repair the dissociative pat-terns in white-bodied folks, we also begin to reshape our collective being as one tethered to the always relational processes of becoming. When we commit to this kind of work, we are committed to the radical acts of embodied liv-ing and embodiment on a cultural scale. This kind of work creates conditions for a chance to rethink democracy from a cultural perspective that allows for us to adapt to a rela-tionality that has the materiality of the body as the primary focus for ways to shape and shift culture.

This allows democracy to be more than a stale model of governance and instead to be a kind of living organism grounded in the politics of embodied relating and embod-ied logic. When we ground and root our politics and our processes of becoming in a relational frame, we partici-pate in the prophetic vision of a different kind of future emerging with us and alongside us. It is in this way that embodiment becomes a vision for democracy. May it be so!

EPÍLOGO

At the eleventh hour, as I was writing the last pages of this manuscript, preparing to send it to the publisher on time and without delay, I was doxxed on Twitter. Doxxing is a way of digitally harassing people by exposing personal information. Doxxing—with its very precise way of harming, harassing, and threatening people—put me in touch with all the pain and suffering that folks experience around ways that white-bodied folks are so dissociated from themselves and the social pain that is the reality on a global scale. I took all the necessary precautions recommended by my social media consultants and security advisors, and though I lost a full week of writing as I dealt with all the necessary security measures required to be implemented (and there were a lot!), I also was deeply in touch with the pain of so many white-bodied folks who participated in this doxxing event. As I mentioned, it happened on Twitter, a social media platform that I've participated in since 2007 and the most abusive relationship I've ever been in. On this platform, there's no ethics of engagement, and there is no real sense of embodied community. There is just discourse. It is as if bodies are just floating machines mitigated by a smartphone. We really have lost our way in a disembodied culture. I want more for us as a people who are struggling to get free. I want us to body our feelings in a way that might create conditions for emancipatory visions of what is possible!

The event brought me back to the reason I started writing this book—why I felt it was important to talk about bodies and the ways we've been disembodied and the ways that the culture of whiteness requires white-bodied folks to be dissociated from themselves, to literally cut off their ancestry and their history to participate in a disembodied culture. Though I was harassed and threatened and my personal information was shared, I felt a sense of compassion for not just these folks on Twitter but the thousands of people who are struggling under a long history of being conditioned to be disconnected from their bodies and the call for white-bodied folks to have more than talking points about racism and being antiracist. Of course, I was scared that someone might show up at my front door—just as I was nervous about the packages that were sent to my house after Charlottesville in 2017—but I was in touch with the compassion and the suffering. I held the both/and in my body and wanted a different world. I still want a different world.

For me it was a really clear moment, as though I could picture it all in my hive mind. I could see and sense and feel the struggle of white-bodied folks, even the struggles I've endured in acquiescing and assimilating into whiteness in the academy and whiteness within culture. And seeing is part of the work. And I know that it is not all of the work. Without a vision, as Proverbs 29:18 teaches us, people will perish, and right now, I think we are collectively looking for a vision, and so few of us realize that the vision we are seeking demands a diversity of tactics—a multiplicity of voices and the politics of radical difference. The vision we need is one that facilitates difference so that emancipatory politics can emerge. This vision must be polyvocal and must be grounded in a generative relationality.

In 2013, when three Black women (often referred to by white supremacy culture as radical Black organizers) created a Black-centered political project called Black Lives Matter, I watched the world around me wrestle with what was emerging. Now Black Lives Matter is a member-led global network I find to be a theoethical framework—helping us all reshape and reframe our anthropological imagination. And that's why it's important to say "Black lives matter": so much of our anthropological imagination is tied up in whiteness and accelerates a culture of whiteness. And yet!

In March 2020, when Breonna Taylor was assassinated by the state, we see why, once more, we must say "Black lives matter." And then again, on May 25, 2020, when George Floyd was murdered by Minneapolis police officers, another execution by the state, we suddenly awakened a little bit more and took to the streets on a global scale in the middle of a raging global health pandemic. We could literally feel the loss. And white-bodied folks finally began to wake up a little. I mention this because the body becoming feels the pain, remembers the loss and grief that communities of culture have endured for decades and generations. This is why generational trauma exists, because white-bodied systems have accelerated harm against the least of these.

And so, as I sat with my own panic and anxiety about being doxxed, I was reminded of how much harm and pain exist on a global scale. I was reminded that we need better relationships with ourselves so that we can have better relationships with others. This is why cultural work is so vital. Because entire communities are being harmed by white-bodied systems. This is why we need a better, more robust vision for democracy—because Black lives matter.

The mention of Black death and Black pain shouldn't have to be made to ask people to do better and be better. And I realize that because of the machinations of white-bodied supremacy culture and the patterns of dissociation, white-bodied folks are unable to get in touch with their felt sense of their own bodies, much less the cultural body, whose refrain is one of complex pain and embodies a history of complex trauma. And from my own cultural background, seeing children from Latin America separated from their parents and caged reminds me that in a different time, my life might have looked profoundly different. I am in touch with the pain of a people, the pain of myself in relationship with others, and the pain of the land that we are on. Creation groans, and I join in that groan along with so many others calling for another possible world.

This book doesn't do everything, I know. I believe it does something in extending a deep invitation to you as readers to get into your bodies. I'm known to say that "relationships will save us," and one of the saving relationships we need to cultivate is the relationship we have with our bodies so that we can have a relationship with other bodies. Relating together with deep postures of welcome can actually shift the cultural body—a sign that another possible world is on the horizon. In the words Gloria Anzaldúa taught me, "May we be the healing of the wounds." And so many of those wounds are also lodged into white-bodied persons, which then impact Black and Brown folks. Let us find the connective tissue within ourselves that creates conditions for better relationships with our bodies so that we can envision a more robust, participatory, multivocal democracy centered in difference that lives and breathes politics and policies that embody life-affirming systems where all of us are participating in the healing of the wounds and the woundedness! Ashé.

A MORE PERFECT UNION

Stories of Embodiment in Community

I've been thinking, *How can we become a more perfect union?*

Each July, I am excited because at the end of the month, my birthday magically appears. I celebrate the entire month. And I always dread the Fourth of July. July 4, 1776, was an unfulfilled promissory note by those who fled England on a quest for the separation of church and state. As we've seen over the past several months, years, and decades, each of our relationships to whiteness and our proximity to whiteness complicates our ability to become that perfected union that the Declaration of Independence hinted at. How do we make right on that unfulfilled promise? How do we look to the margins of the margins, invite their voices into this sphere of becoming a more perfect union, and balance the tables so that all are counted as good in a disenfranchised union that is still trying to find its footing? How do we destabilize the center and the bleeding periphery so that we have a more perfect union? I don't know the answers to these questions, but I hope my spirit of wondering encourages you, the reader, to ask similar questions.

If the margins of the margins have been crying out, what will it take for us to hear them in a way that can make the necessary changes that actually result in the material changes our union so desperately needs? Cries for defunding the police or abolishing ICE and prisons are all in one refrain at this moment, but what do we do to actually make the changes that we need? Do we have the capacity to listen to one another and actually hear the pain that we each embody? Are we in touch with the suffering that surrounds us? From those who are without walls and homes to those who are in search of their next fix? Can we hear one another without judgment and with a heart of compassion so that we can become the healing of the wounds?

It was Frederick Douglass who offered us so many insights into progress and freedom. I want to offer some of them here so that we can keep our eye on what so many were fighting for before this current iteration of struggle emerged, adapted, and became what it is today. One of my favorite quotes from Douglass is "If there is no struggle, there is no progress." We must keep moving forward, inciting a revolution of values. This is why I think getting our hands dirty in the world will help mobilize a revolution of values. He calls us to account once more with this biting quote: "Those who profess to favor freedom, and yet depreciate agitation, are men who want crops without plowing up the ground." How can we tend to the gardens of our own lives and make a way where there is no way? He also writes,

"America is false to the past, false to the present, and solemnly binds herself to be false to the future." Can we see a future out of this fragile state of democracy and into a flourishing and more perfect union?

"I prayed for twenty years," he writes in another reflection, "but received no answer until I prayed with my legs." It's time to get our hands dirty, y'all! We won't be who we say we are until we get our hands and feet dirty digging, composting, in this union called the United States of America. Do we have that imagination for the union that we want? May we be the healing of the wounds. Ashé.

The following vignettes are collected out of an impassioned ask to share about the body and embodiment. Knowing that my voice carries essential weight, I wanted to add in other voices to texturize my theory with a more fleshly narrative. I believe conversation and contemplation create conditions for another possible world, and in my attempt to destabilize the single narrative, I asked friends and colleagues to write on bodies and embodiment so that we can have a fuller picture of what is at stake and what is possible. These stories reflect struggle and call us into a more perfect union. May they resonate with you as they do with me each time I read them!

MADELEINE LOHMAN | SHE, HER

There is a quote from James Joyce that reads, "Mr. Duffy lived a short distance from his body." By puberty, I was very familiar with that distance. Earlier than my classmates, I grew bigger, curvier, and hairier. My parents saw my distress and took it upon themselves to save me from my body. They'd hijack me from high school lacrosse practice and drive me right to diet clinics like Jenny Craig or Nutrisystem without telling me where we were going. I got the message loud and clear—my body was a liability, best avoided when possible.

In my midtwenties, at the cusp of understanding my Queer identity, I went with my first love for a picnic by Lake Washington. As we waded into the water, I suddenly froze. It was as though a wall had been slammed down between my body and me. I couldn't feel the water, or the love I had for my partner, or the joy I expected from such a moment. It was like my emotions were paralyzed.

The best gift I've ever received to guide me toward my own embodiment was my bipolar II diagnosis. It's shown me that any distance I thought I could keep from my body was a harmful illusion. If my mind could have managed my illness on its own, it would have done so long ago. It turns out my mind, body, and spirit are so completely interdependent that unraveling one from the other no longer makes sense. Talk therapy and medication were one vital aspect of my treatment, but they really started to take hold when I added yoga, movement, learning about body liberation, and the possibility of rejecting social norms about what I should look like and who I should love.

For me, embodiment is a deep listening to the cycles of our human form. It's letting, as Mary Oliver says, "the soft animal of your body love what it loves." It can feel incredibly vulnerable.

Here in Northern California—where I moved when I realized the low, gray skies of the Pacific Northwest were contributing to my depression—we are now moving into late fall and winter, and the shortening of the days awakens old melancholy in me. Well-worn habits of wanting to check out arise, a desire to distance myself from the pain and sadness of a human life. To not abandon my body in these moments is a challenge I don't always rise to. But I truly believe in the value of trying. I believe at the heart of this integration of body, mind, and spirit is a vast potential of unconditional kindness and radical self-love.

DANI FISCHER | THEY, THEM

"It's complicated" is more than a phrase used to describe one's romantic relationship status on Facebook. Honestly, I cannot think of a better way to describe my relationship to my body than those two words. I, of course, am not unique in this sentiment. The relationship between a person and their body has long been a subject of interest—thanks so much for that, white supremacy, capitalism, and the patriarchy—I super appreciate your obtrusive and unrelenting efforts to make me believe that I am only worthy if I meet a very specific vision of the binary. I say these things almost cavalierly, which is me putting up my armor, because for me, the refrains of "It's OK, you just have good child-bearing hips" are a hallmark of comments that haunt my relationship with my body. This comment first said to me when I was a teenager—*a teenager!!!*—and subsequently said to me again in my adulthood, as my weight fluctuated, is not an uncommon platitude; raise your hand if you have ever been told "You have good child-bearing hips" or any other inanity that attempts to justify the way your body looks.

As a genderqueer-identified person and as one who was well into their thirties before really beginning to explore my own understanding and relationship with gender, I could only tell you that those early comments about my body were hurtful, but they were hurtful for different reasons than I had assumed at the time they were said. In all three instances where those words were lobbed at me, they were said by people with whom I had significant relationships, and I believed they were hurtful for the reason that most persons assigned female at birth, in a society that centers on the white Euro-Western ideal of femininity, would think they were hurtful; they were a euphemism for fat, and fat, according to society, was not desirable. So in response to each of those instances, I bought into toxic diet culture, chasing the elusive ideal that I would never meet in an attempt to conform to society's standards.

In an attempt to find my place and become comfortable with my body I experimented with multiple paths, from fad diets, to trying to dress in more flattering ways for my "feminine" body, to attempts to find support and community within circles of predominantly feminine or female-identified spaces, as that was what was deemed appropriate. Like, I love the concept of body positivity, believe me, I do; however, I have never felt like the body positivity community was a place I belonged or would be accepted. In all fairness, I have never made any attempt to join that community, and that assumption is based solely on my observations while scrolling social media, so maybe I would belong? I don't know. I think part of my struggle there is that I feel like the predominant discourse and representations of body positivity are ones focused on folks who are female identified and—spoiler—that is just not me. Again, not a knock against anyone who believes in and/or is a part of the BoPo movement; it was just another avenue that I explored in an attempt to feel embodied that didn't meet what I needed.

My relationship with my body has always been complicated, clearly, as demonstrated by the experiences above, but in the past ten years, I have been able to uncover the root of that complication. It is not because my body doesn't meet a certain feminine ideal. In truth, what I discovered was that my relationship with my body was complicated because when I looked in the mirror, my "child-bearing hips" were incongruent with the masculine appearance that I saw myself as in my head. When I finally came to terms with this, it fundamentally shifted what I wanted from my body and the way I would go about becoming and being embodied.

What I have learned is that becoming embodied, for me, has been as much about what happens between my ears, as that is what has allowed me to find my place and feel embodied in a way that works for me. I have learned that I need movement, not for my body, but for my mind, to quiet the voice that wants to pick apart and perseverate about all the ways in which my body does not meet what society says it should be on either side of the binary and certainly in between. Movement—vigorous, intense movement—is my key to being embodied; it is in that vigorous and intense movement that I find my equilibrium. I move to feel the ache of my tired muscles, as that reminds me of my humanity.

TRISTAN TAORMINO | SHE, HER

I spend a lot more time in my head than I do in my body. I get lost in there with all the memories, images, ideas, plans, and a scrolling to-do list that never ends. I rarely ever stop thinking. My brain can be both a comfortable place (when I feel curious, creative, and confident) and a destructive one (when I feel dark, depressed, and hopeless).

Raised under white supremacy and capitalism with puritanical values, there are rewards for thinking a lot, especially when the thoughts lead one to produce. I've been hyperproductive for most of my life. Through years of therapy, I realized that overworking was my form of self-harm because I did it at the expense of my mental and physical health. What was confusing was that my self-harm (unlike other behaviors with the same label) led to what is considered success by the dominant culture. Exploitation was an inside job all along.

I've been taught by society's institutions that mind and body are a binary, and you are in one or the other; it's taken a long time for me to undo those constructs and see the mind and body—my mind and body—as one intimately connected, interdependent being. I originally turned to Buddhism and meditation for self-preservation: to quiet my mind, become more present, and find balance. In meditation, we are taught to focus on the breath. Acknowledge the thoughts, let them float by, and just breathe. It's a simple idea, but it can be grounding and soothing and also be unbelievably difficult and frustrating. When I notice and concentrate on my breath, my brain often has other ideas; it wants to go back to thinking. But when I am really present, my mind takes a break and focuses only on my inhale and exhale. Inhale. Exhale. Meditation is what ultimately led me back to the process that keeps me alive and in my body.

It's ironic what a fraught relationship I have with my body, since bodies are an integral part of my job. I am a sex educator who talks about how bodies are sites of knowing and of shame, of pleasure and of resistance. I teach people (and myself, as teachers do) how to learn, accept, heal, and celebrate our corporeal forms. The first step: we have to acknowledge them as they are, then we have to spend more time really being in them, which is harder than it sounds.

When I come into my body, I can feel grounded, connected to the Earth. But sometimes it's not a good feeling—especially when I am fired up to do something physical that is beyond my body's capabilities. Living in a body with pain makes it even harder to want to stay there, and pain takes many forms. There is the searing pain of my nerves being pressed on by the disks in my spine; back pain is all-encompassing, and I often feel sliced into disembodied pieces like a lady in a magician's box. The pain fluctuates, cascades, but it's always there. The trick is to forge ahead without being put back together.

When I am depressed, I'm in a different kind of pain. I turn anger and sadness inward, and I abandon my breathing form, I pretend it's not there. I deprive it of care. During these times, my body is not my temple, as the saying goes. I don't feed it or clean it. I don't cherish or love it. I'm in pieces again.

Embodiment is about translating my beliefs and values into practice and being mindful of how my body moves through the world. To live in my white body is to acknowledge its privilege: it protects me from racism, affords me unearned value over other bodies, and is less likely to be criminalized. That sits beside the truth that inhabiting my body is a practice of both radical acceptance and subverting norms. I can't escape the Christian notion that the body and mind are prone to sin and filth. I enjoy both. My body is fleshy and hungry, qualities women are not encouraged to embody. I've used my sexualized body to earn money in a whorephobic society. I appear able-bodied but live with two invisible disabilities. I've had to learn to listen to and respect my body when health care professionals will not. My body seeks Queer sex, pleasure, and love in a life outside heteronormativity and mononormativity. This vessel of skin and bones can't do everything I want it to. I don't always trust it, nor it me. Being in a body is a process. I am in that process.

Inhale, exhale.

JEFFREY KOETJE, MD | HE, HIM

"From my cunt."

As if to retroactively hear better what I *thought* I had just heard, I leaned in over the outdoor café table that I and my two dining companions had occupied for the better part of two hours; obviously, this Sunday brunch conversation was about to get even more interesting. Had I known in advance that this delicious truth *bombe* would be the dessert course, I might not have so thoroughly devoured the Jengaesque mound of chicken and waffles that had been placed in front of me an hour earlier.

My dining companion who delivered this mouth-puckeringly sharp re*torte* is a Trans person, in response to a question posed by our other dining companion, a woman-loving woman elder in the movement for racial justice and civil rights. So right away, I knew this answer, flippant as it may have sounded on the surface, went far deeper, reaching a fleshy truth with the precision of a glacé surgical knife. The question itself was an interesting one: "Where do you speak from?"—a way of asking, *What is the grounding center of your voice?*

It's a good policy I generally try to follow that what is said and shared between you and me over Sunday brunch should stay between you, me, and the chicken and waffles, but I bent this rule a bit later that week when I shared the anecdote with my psychotherapist, a cis, white, gay male academic whose research and therapy practice focuses on Queer(ing) relationality. The thing is, I couldn't get that question out of my head, because I couldn't really answer it for myself. Where do I speak from? What is the grounding moral center of my voice? I realized I had some work to do, some inward journey of discovery to embark on.

I have formal training in medicine and theology, and having a degree in biology, I felt then and feel now drawn to explore these questions for myself from both physical and metaphysical lines of inquiry. After all, my dining companion had made it very clear that they were not merely speaking metaphorically or metaphysically: they said, "From my cunt," not "*As if* from my cunt." And while I'm no more than a philosophy hobbyist—and admittedly a fairly promiscuous (syncretistic) materialist in my own philosophical orientation—I also know from physics and psychedelics that lots of states of being and lots of matter and subatomic particles remain undetectable—or at least ineffable—because they are an aspect of reality for which we have not yet developed the tools to detect and/or describe them, and perhaps never will, but that doesn't mean they don't exist. For me, the question of *From where do I speak?* draws me inward toward the so-called dark matter of my own materiality: What aspects of my (physical) being and (metaphysical) beingness have for so long gone undetected/undetectable, or unnoticed/unnoticeable, or buried so deep as to *seem* unreachable, or even perhaps not there at all?

Because of the kind of academic training I've received, I am well equipped to engage in critical inquiry about concepts and theories, but—rather ironically, given my medical training—what I have not been well prepared to do is cultivate critical awareness about my own body, about my embodiment. (Formal training in "Western," "evidence-based" medicine is actually an enculturation into dis-embodiment, but I digress.) But this is OK, because at least I have come to recognize my own dis-embodiment and could start and continue a never-ending process of re-embodying myself, of emerging by going deep down inside, asking myself, *Where does it hurt?* (A question I am learning to ask myself and others as modeled by "Mama" Ruby Sales.)

So where did I start in my journey to/ward a re/turn to embodiment? If I am to rediscover/uncover the place(s) of my being from which I speak (my truths), then I must look to the part(s) of my body from which I have been cut off—for it is there, in the dis-memberment, that the pain resides and from which, upon re-membering, my voice strengthens and grows, sending healing vibrations to the wounds hidden within fleshy folds of myself.

And so I started with my own cunt, or, anatomically speaking, I started with my prostate. Because what organ physically and culturally associated with maleness and masculinity is more symbolically and actually cut off from men than the prostate? The prostate is a nugget of tissue onto which all sorts of heteronormative psychosexual anxiety are projected. It contains a network of pleasure nerves that, when fully activated, can make your eyes roll back in your head—multiple times in a row, in fact, but the most direct route of access to the prostate is via the asshole.

Heteronormativity teaches boys and men that above all else, we are not ever to allow ourselves to be penetrated, only to penetrate. This is what misogyny (and its alternate personas, homophobia and transphobia) turned inward can look like: not wanting to "debase" ourselves by accepting even the possibility of penetration, we sever ourselves not merely from an internal organ of unbelievable pleasure, but in dis-membering ourselves, we also become separated from our own humanity. Heteropatriarchy is a grand bargain, and in this grand bargain, we might "get" an *external member* that we are trained to obsess over from birth to death, but that's just the sleight of hand that prevents us from seeing just how much *internal violence* we suffer at our own hands, in severing ourselves from our prostates, in severing ourselves from ourselves, lest we become the thing/state-of-being we have been taught to fear and hate: being dominated.

Heteropatriarchy is a bargain, imposed onto us, and ultimately for most, it's a bargain we come to accept, or become resigned to, or destroyed by even before we have the chance to read the terms and conditions; in cases that are still far too rare, it's a bargain that we come to reject, resist, and rebel against. I grew up an effeminate, bookish, sensitive, quiet boy, the target of bullying from the beginning of kindergarten through the end of high school (my entire primary and secondary education occurred within the walls of a private Christian school system), submerged in a culture of masculinist supremacy, white supremacy, Christian supremacy, and the militarism of right-wing political ideology. In fact, when the mainline Calvinism of my childhood church revealed itself to be too susceptible to "feminizing" forces (ordaining women?!), my parents dragged me and my sister into increasingly "muscular" denominations of fundamentalist and evangelical Christianity at the same time I was coming (cumming) to sense a certain pleasure principle inside of me—what others tried to convince me was an abomination: my budding (homo)sexuality.

Now I find myself in my midforties, actively working to deconstruct the heteropatriarchal terrorizing that I've internalized. *Indeed, I find that I have been penetrated my whole life, in spite of being told never to allow it.* But what I discover upon turning inward is that what has penetrated me has in fact *impaled me*, and how could I possibly speak my truth when both my mouth and my ass are filled with a spike intended to dominate me, silence me, and ultimately kill me?

As so, over the past several years, in the context of a very loving, deeply supportive, and freeing partnership of over twenty years, I have turned inward and downward to/ward the center of my being and have begun to learn to identify where exactly in my body it hurts, where exactly in my body has my body been cut off from me. In re-membering my body, in re/turning to/ward my prostate, my pleasure principle, I am growing a language for what had been forcefully taken from me, the right to feel in my body the (w)hole(ness) of my being and the right to name and express my truths, which is just another way of claiming for myself the universal human right to have Life and to have it abundantly.

There is a song, written by one of my all-time favorite pop groups, Pet Shop Boys, titled "To Speak Is a Sin." It's a song, written in the early 1980s, about the unspoken rules of hooking up in the gay bars prior to the mainstreaming of white gay male culture: "I always thought it was about sad, old, lonely homosexuals not daring to talk to anyone attractive in a bar" (Chris Lowe, in an updated interview). For the men in the song, to speak is a sin, but for me, *not to speak* is damnation. Now a few years into this journey, I am speaking, speaking a language I will always be growing: a language that will never, no matter how enlarged, be able to contain the pleasure of becoming whole again. It's a divine language because it's a language of experiencing pleasure through the (w)hole(ness) and holiness of being. And so, I open myself up, draw deep from the moral center of my being, and let out a *barbaric yawp*; pleasure flows unrestrained and floods the channels that were always meant to let the Pleasure Principle of Life flow. And where there had been mostly pain, now there is, also, so much beauty.

Where do you speak from? Where, inside of you, is the grounding moral center for your voice?

And just as importantly, where does it hurt?

Start there.

Written on Wednesday, January 6, 2021, the day that a mostly male mob of white supremacists, white nationalists, KKK and neo-Nazis, QAnon conspiracists, and Trump regime–supporting seditionists stormed the US Capitol during congressional certification of the Electoral College votes for Joe Biden and Kamala Harris. Notably, the only mob participant to be killed by Capitol Police was a white woman.

JAMES PRESCOTT | HE, HIM

Being fully present, being in my body, knowing my body, has always been a challenge for me. There are multiple reasons for this. I've been through major childhood trauma, emotional and physical. I never learned to love myself.

In fact, the lesson my childhood trauma taught me was that I wasn't valuable and that my body was embarrassing and unattractive.

The other part of my body was my brain. Being on the autistic spectrum, I could be frustrated; I needed order to feel safe, even if intuitively I knew I was safe and things were OK. I was battling with myself.

Add to this being an Enneagram 4 with a 5 wing. Type 4s are deep thinkers, very emotion driven and intuitive. Type 5s are very much in their heads, methodical, logical. It's like having a split personality at times, and they've been constantly at war with one another.

Finally, I am a highly sensitive person. I take in energy and emotion from all around me and internalize it. So in early 2020, as the pandemic hit, I took on all the collective grief and trauma from the whole world and was feeling it in my body. I'd always been a deep thinker, I was often in tune with my inner self, I'd always been vaguely in tune with my intuition. But I didn't have a relationship . . . often this part of me felt out of my control.

I had practices to help me manage this, but my body wasn't in tune.

My word for 2020 had been *embodiment*. But I wasn't sure how this would happen.

Then I found an embodiment coach. In our four months working together, she introduced me to the concept of my body as a person. A he/she/they, not an "it." I began to spend time listening to my body. And not simply in the common sense of paying attention to habits or illnesses or aches, but literally listening.

I also began doing work with a therapist, called Internal Family Systems—IFS—a form of therapy where you go effectively into different parts of your brain and personalize them and literally sit and talk to them and build a relationship with them to help you process trauma and conflict.

So I began listening to and dialoguing with my body. This wasn't just even listening to my intuition—although this was a revelation in itself—it was connecting with what I was feeling or carrying. The energy, emotion, feeling, actions of my body and in my body.

The core truth I was learning was that embodiment is a relationship.

One Sunday during this time, I woke up and immediately felt anger in my body. I had no idea why. I just knew it was in my body.

So instead of reacting, I paused. I took a breath.

Then I remembered it was Mother's Day. My mother had died twenty years before. Although I'd not consciously remembered it was Mother's Day, my body knew—and was expressing grief at not having my mother on Mother's Day. So instead of getting angry, I stopped. I allowed myself to cry. I gave my body permission to grieve.

I also began to get into more dialogue tune with my HSP, my intuition, picking up on the energy of the world. On August 28, 2020, for example, my body knew something was wrong. I knew something bad had happened. I was angry, more than normal, and for no reason. I checked; it wasn't a memorable day, an anniversary, or a meaningful day for me. But I knew it was something.

The next morning, August 29, I woke up to find Chadwick Boseman had died the day prior—but the news had only just broken.

My body knew. My body had picked up the energy of the overwhelming grief and loss the world was about to learn about and internalized it before any of us even knew. So I took time for myself. I sat on my bed, and the tears began rolling gently down my cheeks. I let my body grieve well. For as long as it took.

Again, I was seeing that healthy embodiment is a relationship.

This work also began to help with my autism. I learned to perceive in advance when a situation might be difficult for me, and this allowed me to prepare. I learned to have grace with myself. I talked to my body and to my internal managers in and out of therapy, I listened, I learned, and I built up a good relationship with them.

I was becoming more and more connected to my body. Obviously we had conflicts and disagreements. But I knew myself better. I was listening to my body, dialoguing with him, and my intuitive and head knowledge and connection to my deepest, truest self and everything going on with me were deeper than ever.

Listening to my body became natural, almost like breathing.

The moment I knew this for sure was late 2020, when I did a full-body meditation. Looking at myself in the mirror. The place I couldn't go to before. I spent time looking at myself, at my body, listening, letting everything inside come out. I put my hand on my chest. I physically felt my whole body. I felt a connection to myself fully and completely for the first time. All the work was bearing fruit.

Me and my body then became a team. Working together for our own good, to be our best me. That night I put my headphones on, and me and my body danced together. Partners.

The relationship won't always be this easy. We'll still have our struggles; there's still more work to do. But now I know we're on the same page. When me and my body work together, I'm more fully connected to myself, know myself better, and can deal with conflict and struggle in a much healthier way than before.

Because I've learned that embodiment is a relationship.

PREETA BANERJEE | SHE, HER

After twenty years in academia and consulting, I find myself as the first Hindu advisor in the Tufts University Chaplaincy. This comes with much gratitude for the journey and a responsibility to support others in finding their own paths of calling. Recently, I posted in a reflection regarding "Primary and Secondary Trauma for Healers" by Vahisha Hasan and Brenda Salgado offered as part of the TRACC4Movements Movement Trauma Healing Training.

As Vahisha and Brenda reminded us, secondary trauma is trauma that occurs after repeatedly engaging and empathizing with people who have been traumatized. I identified a need to remember not to talk about practices more than actually practicing. This is how I recognize secondary trauma in my own life—it feels like asking permission or space to be rather than just being.

A dear reader of my post remarked that they also wanted to learn how to practice more than talking about practice. So here is a deeper reflection on my own barriers to embodiment and how I can just practice. Before I explore any further, let me indulge the talking about practicing a little bit longer. To me, practicing means authentically connecting with the Divine through techniques handed down to me through my family, my studies, and my lived experiences. As a Hindu, those techniques include chanting, sitting in meditation, body and breath work, and selfless service (i.e., sacred listening).

To me practicing, more than talking about practicing, requires Trust. Trust in the environment to allow my total immersion in my body and my being. Trust in my body to be able to process all the raw and unprocessed emotions. Trust in the Divine that I only get what I can handle.

In these unprecedented times, it takes more work to embody that Trust. With everything virtual these days and without sensing the physical presence of community practice, it has been hard to feel into reality at times. Honestly, on my own, I am more sensitive to disruptions to my practice, so I don't even start. I often forget that I need to ease into spaces to be vulnerable and to not give myself the time or space.

This is where forgiveness comes in. There is a *subhashitam*, or a wise saying in Sanskrit, that loosely translated says, "Form is an ornament for humans, qualities adorn form, knowledge adorns qualities, forgiveness is the best adornment for knowledge." To me, what this wise saying means is that the body is a beautiful container that is further made beautiful by its qualities and the knowledge that animates the form and qualities. However, without forgiveness, that knowledge, the qualities, and the body remain stuck. Forgiveness is the lubrication that gives us flow.

This is also where remembering comes in. Remembering awakens my body. I am actualized in the continuous presence of a community of ancestors, elements, planets, and people all in support regardless of physical circumstances. Remembering allows me to move beyond my physical senses of touch, taste, sight, smell, and sound to truly know that I am always accompanied. That energy primes the pump of my embodiment.

And this is where clearing comes in. Clearing gives me space to pull forth my practice. It is an ever-present beginning practice to say no. Boundaries are necessary for the fullness of embodiment. Maybe this is why our spiritual beings needed human forms. Emptying myself strengthens my attention to practice. There is almost a vacuum that a clearing of time and space can spontaneously transform into practice.

With forgiveness, remembering, and clearing, I feel my Trust return. I am ready to feel and experience whatever needs to be felt and experienced to be fully embodied, even in fits and starts, even in the messy imperfection of my limitless nature.

As I finish writing this, I find my ancestors growing in number. I feel compelled to close this reflection with the realization that my body is constantly pulled, sometimes torn, between two countries. My DNA and spirit are tied to India, while my mental frameworks and muscles are tied to the United States. I also realize that our embodiment practices must acknowledge that just because immigrants need to declare allegiance to become citizens, it doesn't determine the bodily preferences of their children. My ancestors' connections continue to deepen in me with age, with practice, and with care.

PAM J. ROCKER | SHE, HER

Living with chronic pain for over eight years has completely transformed my relationship with my body. I used to go days or even weeks without thinking anything particular about the way I physically move through the world, but now, the reality of my being requires me to be intentional about every step.

Pain has evolved from the occasional transient ache to a constant deluge of distracting outcries emitting from my body. It is a volume that I once used to be able to control but have now lost the remote.

In the past, when others would divulge that they lived with chronic pain, I wondered if it was anything different than a particularly bad headache that reemerged every few weeks. How naive and pain-free I used to be! I'm ashamed at how glibly I would mutter "I'm so sorry about that" while secretly feeling that if only they made a few different choices in life, they'd get "better," whatever that means.

Now when I meet another person living with chronic pain, I feel like I can look into their eyes, and they'll understand something about me that few others can. They know what it's like to walk through the world with this invisible illness, contorting their movements and activities in order to shape-shift around the pain and not be too bothersome to those around us. They do the same limbic dance that I do, and I'm both sad and relieved when I find a kindred spirit.

Pain is so personal and yet so universal. Doctors ask us to rate it on a scale of one to ten in hopes that somehow we can translate this most intimate feeling into something that people on the outside can quantify. Is it stabbing, achy, tingly, sharp, numbing, shooting, prickly, burning? Yes, usually, thanks for asking.

As much as I would like to glorify my distancing from my body as an act of survival, I know that this is only an illusion. I can't disconnect from the corporeal form that carries me around, and my attempts to do so only cause more pain and confusion in the long run. If I detach, I also lose my connection to my breath, my heartbeat, the sensations that bring me not only pain but also pleasure. The beauty and the dimensionality would also be dimmed. There is no way to compartmentalize the numbing.

In the past eight years, the biggest lie I've been told by Western medicine is that the lack of complete healing is a moral failing. Not only are we taught to be detached from our bodies, to ignore pain, and to never look weak; we are also told to dominate our own bodies by demanding that they recover in our way, in our timeline. There's an assumption that where there is a will, there is a way and that illness or injury can only exist if we're not trying hard enough.

This is where our fixations with "cures" become toxic. The reality is, there are so many things that do not have a cure. Our worship of bodies that appear untouchable, unharmed, cured, or curable can't help but feed the idea that some bodies are worth more than others, and in this equation, unwell bodies are far more disposable. It's no wonder why so many people who live with chronic pain struggle with suicidal ideation. If we require accommodations in a society where deviations from perfection are loathed, what is our societal currency worth?

When I met my acupuncturist several years ago, she asked me to write down what I enjoyed doing. After she read through the long list I had written, she praised me, saying that people who experience the amount of pain I do rarely enjoy anything. I wept right there in her office. It had been so long since I had been celebrated for existing instead of shamed for remaining the same. The label of failure fell from me so hard, I could almost hear it shattering on the floor.

This treasured moment taught me more than anything my specialists told me. I felt permission and prodding to celebrate what I could do, the ways in which I still reached out for pleasure and reached in for meaning. I missed feeling familiar with my body and caring enough to make a lovely home inside of it and suddenly woke up to realize I could still make a warm place for myself, even inside the pain. Whether my pain was at a one or a ten, whether I did one or one hundred things that day or not was irrelevant; the main point was realizing that my body was always lovable enough to deserve my affection and attention. I was still welcome here, soul and body—my whole body—in all of its realness and complexities. In this way, the spirituality of my body and its inherent dignity have finally reconciled with what I believe to be true about all our souls: we are sacred and worthy of belonging. Period.

Sometimes I still feel like my body is a heartless landlord who has been trying to evict me for years. Other times, when the world is quiet and still and I feel my breath roll in waves of nourishment, I recognize that my body is always, in all ways, doing the very best it can, and a rush of tenderness and self-forgiveness overcomes me. I remember the smooth lines and soft curves that make up the sum of me, picture myself in the sexiest outfit I have, and settle into myself like a favorite sweater.

There is no talk of a cure. Nothing needs to be fixed. I become softer and resist the hardness that the world invites me to engage in. In this softness, I am liberated from expectations to heal, yet in this freedom, I do experience a kind of healing. A healing that has nothing to do with getting "better" and everything to do with coming home to myself and being so fiercely kind to myself that I can't help but sit and stay for a while.

ANNA GOLLADAY | SHE, HER

In an encounter recorded in John's biblical Gospel, we turn a story that centers on embodiment into a story that centers on trauma, fear, and, oh yes, doubt. For any of us who have listened to a post-Easter sermon, the theme of doubt is never far from our memories. Thomas was grief-stricken, mourning the death of his friend and leader, even though he's been told that Jesus has risen. Amid this trauma and being absent when Jesus first visits, he wasn't interested in someone's reassurance that the Savior was no longer dead, that they had seen him and he should simply trust them. Instead, he yearned for an embodied encounter with Christ. When Jesus finally appears a week later, he says to Thomas, "Put your finger here and see my hands. Reach out your hand and put it in my side. Do not doubt but believe" (John 20:27). This story of Thomas is so much more than one of doubt. It's a story that illuminates embodiment as a path to healing.

An understanding of—and an ultimate embracing of—embodiment is not one that I've found easy. As a child, I watched my slightly overweight mother be berated continuously by my father. I experienced bullying over my lanky figure and lack of curves. As a young teenager, I survived a painful sexual assault. Later in my teens, my body developed into one that curried me unwanted attention and uncomfortable leers. As an undergraduate, my weight fluctuated, turning the scrutiny of my father's opinion away from my mother. Once married, I started cooking more and lazily enjoying my partner's companionship while both our bodies morphed into shapes that echoed our comfort in one another. I shied away from exercising because someone told me that sweating wasn't a "good look on me." I began experimenting with unexpected and edgy hairstyles to take attention away from my body in my late thirties. For much of my four and half decades, it was hard to recall moments where I've looked in a mirror and affirmed the woman who stares back. I have a hard time remembering days where my body isn't a source of shame and apathy.

All the while, this capsule of bone and organ, skin and fluid, knowledge and energy has accompanied me on the journey of a lifetime. As a seven on the Enneagram, the adventure gene runs deep. As a part of the head triad, I'm always up for an exciting adventure.

While my head and heart thought they were busy doing exotic things, my body was the plus-one on the journey. My body was the carry-on luggage that rolled along behind, never more than an afterthought. What was actually happening was that I was negating my understanding of the whole and therefore missing a critical piece of my journey—the way that others embodied experience alongside me.

My appreciation for my body began to change at some point, but I noticed it first in August of 2017. While walking alongside other faith leaders toward the then named Robert E. Lee Park, I was strikingly aware of my body's vulnerability. While standing in front of the park, holding the line, and receiving threatening actions from Unite the Right supremacists, I thanked my body for its strength. While being spat upon, I thanked my body for its calm. While being yelled at to recite the books of the Hebrew text, lest I be accused of being a pastoral imposter, I thanked my body for its resolve. As I retreated in the height of the violence and my body moved me safely to our meeting point, I thanked it for its energy. On that day in August, I recognized not only the integration of body with heart and mind but also the need for my whole self to engage in the work of liberation.

You see, liberation is unattainable without the body, without the collective. For those of us who ascribe to a Christian faith tradition, it is not coincidental that we are called the body of Christ. In order to interact and experience one another, and God, in full and authentic ways, we have to place our bodies in that space. We have to physically engage in the work of community with the fullness of ourselves in order to denounce our sins of white supremacy, racism, and narcissism. Our capacity to be <u>with</u> one another, to engage with one another in unveiled realism, will bridge our differences in radical ways.

Rowan Williams aptly reminds us that "our identity is being made in relations of bodies . . . [that] we belong with and to each other."

"I have not seen anyone who became more aware of their body in its fragility and grace without also becoming more compassionate to all of life." Broadcaster and author Krista Tippett offers these words to guide conscientious understanding of the barriers we place between ourselves and our capacity to become truly embodied. Our bodies hold within them blended fragility and strength, blended critique and grace, doubt and confidence, trauma and health. The dichotomy of difference is staggering. To move more fully into the strong, graceful, confident, and healthy, we must navigate the fragile, critical, doubtful, and traumatic. There are so many of us with stories like mine—stories that underestimate and minimize our bodies' capacity, stories that amplify the voices of those who matter so little and stifle the voice of self that matters so deeply. We must see our bodies as the conduit to liberation, pushing us to heal, relieving us from doubt. Our collective liberation depends on it.

SHAKIYLA SMITH | SHE, HER

I feel on the verge of a new relationship with my body that I am struggling to enact and grow into. It is connected to issues of aging, mortality, self-love, worthiness, radical acceptance, and identity. And my resistance to all of these things. One weekend last year, I went to get a massage. I was already feeling tender and a bit melancholy. I'm not exactly sure why. However, I also had been reading a book by Roxane Gay, *Hunger*, which is beautiful, brilliant, and brutal. She calls it a memoir of her body, and in it, she describes in clear, intimate language her experience of living in a Black, six-foot-three, 450-pound "undisciplined" body. She also talks about how society reacts to someone in her body, about our collective fear and hatred of fat and "undisciplined" bodies. I cried while reading her words. At their stark beauty and truth. They surfaced many things for me, including my own fear of having an "undisciplined," 450-pound body. Roxane writes distinctly, "This book, *Hunger*, is a book about living in the world when you are not a few or even forty pounds overweight. This is a book about living in the world when you are three or four hundred pounds overweight, when you are not obese or morbidly obese but super morbidly obese according to your body mass index, or BMI." I am about twenty-five to thirty pounds heavier than my ideal weight, not even necessarily what anyone would consider overweight, though I am now considered overweight according to the BMI. Still, Roxane is not writing about my kind of body. And I understand that there is a vast difference in our embodied experiences. Yet where we connect is around our shared fear of and discomfort around having an "undisciplined" body that then signals your unworthiness—her through her lived experience of actually living in a Black, six-foot-three, 450-pound "undisciplined" body and me as the participant in and recipient of unforgiving cultural messages around beauty and bodies. In fact, she describes an experience and fate that collectively American women are killing themselves to avoid—regardless of size and the actual bodies they inhabit. As a student of feminist thought and body image, I knew this struggle. But this time, I felt it deeply alive in me. It broke me open.

In any case, I spent most of my massage session crying: the twenty minutes before I was even on the table as my massage therapist, who I also practice yoga with, and I shared our experiences of aging and our suddenly "undisciplined," uncooperative bodies, and then the remaining thirty-five minutes that I was on the table. It felt good to let the tenderness and vulnerability of me ooze out—to be emotionally and physically held as I expressed my grief and sadness over my perceived state and experience of my body. How I don't feel the same in it and how my yoga poses don't feel the same—not as strong or open or light. How I almost don't recognize myself, even though the changes to many would be mostly unnoticeable or minimal. How I struggle to accept myself even though I believe in body positivity and believe that women should be allowed to take up space and love themselves fully in whatever body they inhabit. How I feel ridiculous for being vain and worrying about something so superficial. I cried it out as she massaged deeply into my scapula and stretched my arm over my head. In that moment, I encountered the complex, contradictory truth of my body—that I am ashamed of it and that it can also feel deeply, including the pleasure of being touched. I *am* fully alive in my body. We belong to each other. Thankfully. Afterward, I went to a women's self-defense class at a boxing gym, where I honored the strength of my body as it is and practiced kicking, punching, and yelling "No" and "Stay back."

I have spent most of my adult life in a strong, athletic body. I have never wanted to be thin, per se. I prefer a svelte but muscular, fit-looking body for myself. I come from a culture that values curves and thick thighs and round asses. I have been privileged to inhabit such a body, which I developed and maintained through a mostly unprocessed, vegetarian diet since my teens and an active lifestyle—West African dancing since college, a vigorous yoga practice started in my thirties, weekly roller-skating, and hiking. I have lived an intentionally healthy lifestyle that felt mostly effortless and natural, and I never worried much about my weight. Of course, I had the usual minor concerns about perceived flaws and imperfections that plague many women. But for most of my adulthood and particularly my thirties, I felt good and content in my body. I loved the way it felt to stretch backward into my favorite yoga pose—my back curved like the opening of a C, held in an arch by my two feet and one arm, while my other arm stretched through the air toward the ground. I felt simultaneously light and strong. Free. I loved dancing barefoot in rhythm to the chorus of syncopated drums, my hips rotating one way with my legs and arms lifting another. All of my activities were more about how they made me feel physically and emotionally. It was never just physical activity; it was about joy, fun, community, and challenge. I liked the strength and thickness of my thighs, the chisel of my arms, the roundness and lift of my ass, which took years to appreciate and grow into. I felt young and supple, though I didn't really know that that is what I felt. Until I didn't anymore.

Over the past couple of years, I have noticed a shift. Slowly at first and then more pronounced as various life experiences came with it. Graduate school. Relationships ending. Parental caretaking. Job changes. Health challenges. A cross-country move. I still maintained a mostly unprocessed, vegetarian diet and my active lifestyle, with some changes to accommodate the life changes. But something is different.

A couple of years ago, I struggled with extreme fatigue and heart spasms that defied diagnosis. One night, I almost passed out in a movie theater and had to be taken to the emergency room. It was the first time I legitimately thought I would die. I had every relevant test in the world done and pursued all related specialists—including an herbalist and medical intuitive—and no one could figure out the riddle of my body. By all accounts, I was basically the picture of health. Yet I often struggled to make it through the day without a nap. My brain and thoughts were foggy and slow moving. I was scared to sleep at night, when the heart spasms would mostly occur. I had never experienced my body so out of my control and seemingly immune to my intervention. So "undisciplined."

It has been humbling, to say the least. And shameful. With my usual and current mindset, I must be doing something wrong—not exercising enough, not eating correctly. There is no possible way that my body would not respond to my intervention, would be so undisciplined and unruly. And yet here we are.

Lately, though, through sheer despair and the inability to successfully intervene around my body, I have come to the edge of my grief and have met a kind of invitation. An invitation into a new experience and acceptance of my body. An invitation to a kind of radical acceptance and self-love. An invitation into a more feminine, receptive space of not overefforting or overforcing. I find myself skeptical of this invitation and uncertain of what is on the other side of it. And yet there is an invitation, beyond my concerns about my body. And I am curious.

As I enter this new phase of this journey, I encounter different aspects of myself. Shadow sides. Unworthiness. Fear.

Shame. Will I be able to survive and take care of myself if I don't effort? Will I be taken care of? Will I be loved . . . as I am? In the undisciplined and unruly body that I have now, with the foggy mental capacity that I have now? I feel that there is something on the other side of this. Yet I don't know what it is. And there is also the possibility that there isn't.

REFLECTION AND SOMATIC OFFERING

BY ERIN C. LAW

I'm honored to get to share my thoughts on this complex terrain of bodies, democracy, supremacy culture, social healing, the change process, and becoming in light of my background in dance, creative arts, somatics, bodywork, and cultural studies. This is work related to my call and vocation: to facilitate educational spaces rooted in creative embodied practices that support people and communities who are ready and willing to compost supremacy culture and lean into collective liberation.

In the pages that follow, I'll begin by offering my perspective and reflection on Robyn's rich and textured writing. Then the text will move into a somatic invitation, an offering you might play with, practice, and shape as it best suits you. Finally, I'll leave you with a story and some questions about the collective healing of our democratic body. Throughout this text, you'll meet an invitation to check in with your body, noticing the subtle responses and sensations you might have as you read and continue to process all you have read up to this point.

REFLECTION

In this emerging field of cultural somatics (as coined separately but with parallel timing by Resmaa Menakem and Tada Hozumi), we are often following curiosities about how healing practices used in "traditional" therapeutic one-on-one settings might serve the entire cultural body as we seek social and collective healing.

What we call *somatics* and *embodiment* today is often cut off and removed from a way of being that emerged from Indigenous cultures around the world. These cultures had (and still have) particular ways of connecting with themselves, each other, their communities, and their environments that promoted "right relationships" with all that is. As my mentor, Elisheva Wolff (they/them), often reminds me, if we go back far enough in our ancient lineage, all of us have ancestors who practiced this way. Integrating "head, heart, and body" would be irrelevant in our ancient ancestors' times because they lived from their fullness, from a place of deep integration and interconnection to the cycles and mysteries of the planet. So this way of being is right here (in our blood!), available and accessible right now—we just need to lift the veil that has been draped over our consciousness all this intervening time. As I write this in 2021, we continue to awaken and emerge from the wreckage of white colonial violence toward and erasure of these cultures' practices, and those investing in the democracy of the body are desperately searching to practice (and live) differently.

In Indigenous cultures, these practices were a given: they were part of the fabric of everyday living in generative, healthy communities. And now, in the last few decades, we see white men claiming they have invented the embodiment techniques and methodologies that have been around for eons, with many of these practices originating with cultures of color. What's more is that these "new" techniques are often being applied to individuals in a one-on-one therapeutic context, emphasizing healing as an individual process. While individualized therapy and somatics sessions can be incredibly supportive, life changing, and even life-saving, they can also lead toward a tendency to pathologize the individual while disregarding how larger systemic dysfunction has caused harm, pain, and disconnection, even as they apply therapies that are meant to be part of larger community healing practices. I wonder how US culture might shift if we sought to make more explicit connections between our individual well-being and the ways in which the toxicity of our disembodied culture has shaped us all collectively, culturally, and systemically.

My teachers Dare Sohei and Tada Hozumi have written, spoken, and taught on community healing and embodiment. Both of them are humans of color, brilliantly working in and shaping the field of cultural somatics, and have been incredibly generous in that, while they highlight the colonial and white appropriation of and benefit from "own-ing" or "originating" techniques that are not actually theirs, they continue to invite white folks to participate in Indige-nous practices, suggesting that those who do bring a sense of humility, knowing we may not ever fully understand the context and meaning of the cultures from which these practices originated. These teachers understand that on a cultural level, if we want to be in right relationships with anyone or anything, we must engage in different practices than the ones that led us to this disembodied fate. And that is all of us—white, Black, Indigenous, Brown, and people of color—we are all swimming in the murky waters of suprem-acy culture together.

Many people find a way "in" to their bodies through the practice of yoga. And in that presence of humility, I wonder if we might take a yoga class admitting there is so much we may not know about the culture from which this practice originated. Can we expand our capacity to sit within that cultural tension while we simultaneously learn to prac-tice being present with our bodies in crucial ways? During the height of the Delta variant outbreak in India, my col-league Tina Strawn asked her social media followers, "If we enjoy anything at all or benefit in any way from yogic prac-tices, can we now demonstrate our support in India's time of need?" She said that this is not about pity, but she won-dered, "How can we show our empathy, compassion, repa-rations, and action?" It's challenges like Tina's that invite us into community, or as Robyn offers, to be *en conjunto*. It extends a chance to feel connection throughout our global body. With the parts of our cultural body that are closer in geographic proximity, I also wonder how we might connect more intentionally.

OFFERING: AN INROAD TO SOMATIC PRACTICE

After *thinking* through embodiment and *imagining* how that may be an inroad to heal our democracy in and through Robyn's writing, I wonder if for many of us, the next questions are,

> How do we physically practice, and what moves do
> we make?
> What is "the work" of embodiment?
> How do we turn inward toward ourselves so that we
> may heal our democracy?
> What are the practices that may facilitate and mate-
> rialize this change?

Sometimes it can feel overwhelming to consider exactly how we each might be part of the systemic change we want to see—where do we start? I am reminded of adrienne maree brown's phrase "small is all," inviting us all to intentionally take the next best and manageable step toward the change we want to see manifest. If fractals are self-repeating iterative patterns happening on a dynamic spectrum from the micro to the macro—if, as brown says, "what we pay attention to grows"—then which fractals do we want to reiterate? I wonder if being bodied is living with awareness of relational, fractal, and iterative change. You might want to ask yourself what needs to be tended in yourself, your life, your community, and your town or city. What is uniquely yours to do? What's in your lane?

What follows is a description of my process as I digest and integrate the powerful stories, images, and ideas of this book. I invite you to participate in this process with me, with no expectation about how this may go. Maybe you join me for all of this or maybe just for whatever parts resonate the most. In fact, that is the first part of my process: consent. Elisheva Wolff taught me about this practice, this way of being they call "radical consent." With each invitation or interaction, we listen to our bodies for a yes, maybe, or no and follow accordingly. Our compass bodies are so intelligent; they speak of our desires and repulsions and everything in between, if we listen. Opening spaciousness in my solar plexus and diaphragm: yes. Throat tightening, closing, heat flushing in: no. A subtle fluid streaming through my spine: yes, and . . . My inhale and exhale growing shorter in duration: maybe . . . pay attention . . . where is this going?

First, I bow to all my teachers, including my students and clients, whom I also see as my teachers. I bow to the lineages of healing practices from my own blood ancestors and the ancestors of the lineages I have studied. I bow to the land and to all the first people who stewarded this place where I now get to live, acknowledging that I enjoy all the fruits of their labor.

Then I ask myself the questions below; you're invited to ask yourself too. We might even ask, then close our eyes, and if it feels right, take a breath into our bellies and out of our mouths and listen. What are the subtle messages our bodies are whispering to us? Feel free to play with the questions that make you feel most alive.

> Is it possible, in this moment, to notice the sensations
> present in my body?
> What do I feel, think, sense, and imagine after taking
> in the stories in this book?
> What is the texture of my heart?
> What color is my gut?
> Can I feel the back surface of my body?
> Can I feel whatever support is underneath me,
> coming to meet me where I am, unconditionally?
> Does my skin feel close to my fascia, or stretched
> silky and thin and wide, or . . . ?
> What can I feel and where?
> Where is there aliveness?
> Where is there nothing? Numbness?
> Are there sounds I need to make?
> What is my felt sense of the future, the world I
> long to inhabit? What does it look like, feel like,
> smell like, taste like? If I could imagine fifty, one
> hundred, or five hundred years into the future,
> what do I desire to see? How do I imagine people
> relating with one another?

Maybe now, after feeling and sensing what comes up for us in response to these questions, we even draw or paint or dance or write. Maybe we need to go outside and walk or feel the air on our skin. Can we listen to the messages of our bodies and follow accordingly?

We can take all the time we need and come back when we're ready. Maybe you want to put this book down now and take care of yourself. Whatever you want to do, go do that. When you're ready to come back, I'll be here.

Welcome back. How do you feel now? What is alive for you in this moment?

As you take in this last section, I invite you to stay connected to this experience. Can you read with your whole body? What do you notice about where you might be relaxed or holding tension? How is your breath from sentence to sentence?

It seems to me the "work" of somatics is about awareness. Can I hold compassionate awareness for myself while opening my attention to others and the world around me? Is it possible that when I honor my body more attentively, I might be better able to tend to others around me? What if we all did this?

MERGING WITH OUR DEMOCRATIC BODY

I close with an invitation to let ourselves feel the sensations and textures of hope in our tissues, our bones, and maybe even our cells. Can we get really clear about what that feels like in our bodies? I believe deeply that we are interconnected in many ways, some of which we may not even know. If this is true, then my body's journey is parallel to yours. We have a responsibility to tend to our own wounds, to expand our capacity to be with each other through difference, and to plant the seeds we want to see blossom and flourish in our collective garden.

I want to share the story of "We Walk with Shawn" that emerged here—I write this from Cherokee, Shawnee, and Yuchi ancestral land in so-called Nashville, Tennessee—in 2020 during the racial uprisings. A Black man named Shawn wanted to take his daily walk around the neighborhood in which his family had lived for decades. Given the historic terror and fear with which Black folks have lived every day of their lives, let alone the recent deaths of George Floyd and, in this case, Ahmaud Arbery, Shawn's fear was amplified.

Due to sheltering in place, the collective consciousness of the nation was in some ways forced to see the truth about racial violence, which many advantaged groups never have had to consider. So when Shawn voiced his anxiety in an online group, people listened and rallied around him. His neighbors came in droves to accompany him on his walk, where he would some days be flanked by as many as three hundred people. He envisioned this happening across the nation, inviting a walk to take place in Philadelphia and other cities. When I watch the videos of these walks, I am reminded of the ways in which birds flock, with deep intention to stay together throughout the unpredictable twists and turns of their journey. Can you imagine how this might feel to be surrounded and supported by a communal body like this?

Our animal bodies crave community in order to make meaning and to be well. In some ways, I think that if we could all learn how to open our awareness to our human flock, if we could physically practice this more than we currently practice harmful, violent, transactional relationality, we might be on a track toward collective well-being. This was a crystallization of community care and, for a moment, exposed the often invisible connective webbing of spirit, revealing we are never truly alone. And this flock may now have dissipated but has left ripples of togetherness and compassion in the air currents that are still cycling and moving through our collective organism.

When we listen to our bodies and take their messages seriously, we can change culture. One practice, one flock at a time, we can re-member this robust, dynamic, and magnificent body to which we all belong. What are some ways you might be able to tap into this flocking energy in your own community? Are there flocks already moving that you might want to join?

ACKNOWLEDGMENTS

Books are dreamed of and imagined in relationship, and books don't materialize outside of relationships. Relationships with ideas, relationships with narrative, and relationships with people. As such, I'd like to mention the primary relationships that have created conditions for this book.

Several years ago, I knew that my work in the world was to be captured primarily in long-form writing, and in order to be taken seriously by publishers, I needed an agent. While I had talked with several agents, none of them compelled me. After all, it's a business, and what I needed and what I wanted was to be in relationship with an agent, not to have empty transactions with an agent. So I texted a dear friend who has years of experience in publishing and runs a literary consulting practice with her partner. I texted this friend asking if she would be my agent, and her reply was one of needing to discern whether that was even something she wanted to do or had the capacity to do. That friend's name is Cathleen Falsani, and after several years of discernment and even some literary consulting with me, she agreed to agent for me and focus a very selective agenting practice on LGBTQIA+ writers, since many of us have a hard time finding an agent in the world of religious and spiritual literature. Cathleen has been a true godsend to me and my partner as I have journeyed with the book that you have just read. Not only has Cathleen been present to all of my questions, but she has also advocated for me in ways that only a friend can do. During the process of pitching the book, writing the book, and editing the book, Cathleen has stood by cheering me on like a beloved family member would do. I couldn't have imagined this book, pitched this book, or finished this book without Cathleen by my side. She has breathed new life into me and helped me believe that I have something to say and can use story to say it. I owe Cathleen another bottle of Yola Mezcal, and I look forward to seeing her to hug her neck and to thank her as soon as I'm back in California!

Another vital part of the writing process is one's relationship with one's editor. I got very lucky with this book and had the distinct honor and privilege to work with Lil Copan, someone who had reached out to me several years prior soliciting a book from me. At the time, I was just finishing *Activist Theology* and wanted to take time to let things simmer and marinate and see what, if anything, I wanted to write. Little did I know that Lil would circle back around and become the editor for this book. As a first-generation college student and the first in my family to earn a PhD, I always wanted someone to take me seriously. And Lil not only took me seriously but engaged in my work in a real way that really made the book what it is today! I couldn't have written a better book about my own struggle to get into my body without Lil's help. At each step of the way, she was kind and generous, and I think we really became friends throughout this process. Lil is also a writer, and she brought her gift of the craft of writing to bear on this project, and I am eternally grateful for all Lil did for me in the very beginning stages during the pitch process to make this book what it is now. I can only hope to work with Lil again as I explore other topics of translating theory to action and theology to praxis. Lil's insightful wisdom has truly made *Body Becoming* a living, fleshly narrative that returns to the body at each fold.

My doctoral advisor, Dr. Ted Vial, has been another primary supportive relationship as I have emerged as a public scholar and intellectual activist. He and I remain in conversation, read together, and imagine how theological education can be liberative to all. Ted believed in me at a crucial time when I didn't know if I would be able to finish my PhD program or have a committee to see my dissertation through to completion. Ted picked up the pieces and championed me through my process, and still today, he champions me. We text frequently when I'm thinking about something and share a bourbon and scotch when we are in person together, usually at conferences. Ted has been and continues to be an amazing *Doktorvater*, and his support heals a multitude of wounds.

Similarly, Dr. Edward Antonio, who I write about early in the book, has played an important role in my intellectual life. I aspire to be a thinker like him and remain grateful that we keep in touch despite the miles. Edward and I share similar histories but from really disparate realities. He has channeled trauma into thinking complexly, and I have channeled trauma in similar ways. Edward helped me make sense of Deleuze and so many theorists, and his deep posture of welcome is something that continues to buoy me to this day.

I left Texas to study with a Latin American feminist theologian. My professors at Hardin-Simmons University, Dr. Dan R. Stiver and Dr. Robert Sellers, encouraged me to continue to graduate school. I didn't know what that meant, so I researched what graduate school is. That was before Google was a verb! After successfully applying and being admitted to Garrett-Evangelical Theological Seminary, I was introduced to Argentine theologian Dr. Nancy Elizabeth Bedford. The first question she ever asked me is where I went to church. She is concerned with community and relationship, and her theology and ethics are grounded in the same. In many respects, she is my *Doktormutter*. Though she did not supervise my doctoral dissertation, she did supervise my master's thesis, then promptly kicked me out of the nest so that I could learn to fly on my own, so that I might engage my own becoming and learn how to navigate and negotiate *nepantla* as a NonBinary Transgender Latinx. Nancy is one of the most thorough teachers I know, bringing students alongside her and companioning them, and me, along the way. She continues to companion me as I do the work of politicized theology and public ethics in

Babylon. She also was the one who invited me to be faithful in the small things, and my work in the public square is my attempt to be faithful in the small things.

My academic partner, who I mentioned earlier in the book, told me that imagination is the best thing we have on our sides, and Dr. Nikki Young continues to share with me the wisdom that she embodies as she cheers me on in my vocation of being a public scholar and intellectual activist. I am the scholar I am today because Nikki models embodied scholarship in such a compelling way that I learn and seek to embody my scholarship for another possible world. Like Nikki, I am surrounded by a host of scholars and activists, too many to name, who buoy me in my work. I am grateful for my colleagues in the theological academy American Academy of Religion and the Society of Christian Ethics who help me live out my call and vocation in the public square, along with the many activist colleagues who bring me along in their theories and strategies to help me theologize in sustainable ways. I am grateful to Clinton Wright, a movement activist, who was my security detail in Charlottesville, Virginia. That incident bonded us for life, I think, and we regularly meet and discuss theories and strategies for another possible world. I am particularly grateful to Diana Butler Bass, who has been an informal mentor, as she has navigated the public theology space for a long time. She has modeled how to do public scholarship and has remained generous with her time and energy. I am also grateful to my students at Duke Divinity School, who ask really insightful questions and challenge me to be a better teacher every semester, and I am grateful to have a theological home in the borderland spaces of church, academy, and movements as I attempt to live out my very public call and vocation.

The team at Activist Theology Project is a team I could never imagine being able to work with. Jeff, Anna, Erin, Blake, and Abra each help me lean into the work of activist theology that is deeply informed by a collaborative spirit. Each week, Anna and I record the *Activist Theology Podcast*, and each week, I get another chance to lean into the work of translating theory to action and theology to praxis. I am so grateful she has entrusted me as a partner in the work of social healing. Likewise, Jeff is another really important interlocutor for me. I've known Jeff for twenty years; we went to seminary together at Garrett-Evangelical Theological Seminary. Jeff and I were the only two out LGBTQIA+ persons at the time. We found each other in an unlikely space and place while we were traversing our own individual healing and reconnected in 2015 in Washington, DC, when I was speaking at an event. We have been inseparable since! He is my purse; I take him everywhere! He is my ride or die, and I am indebted to him for his brilliance and his compassion and his continuous invitation for me to live out my work. Erin, my beloved partner, is one of the most patient and compassionate people I know. I have taken her work so seriously that I have committed myself to be in deeper relationship with my body and seek a way out of no way and to live out theology and ethics in such a way that it is deeply embodied with social courage. I couldn't have written a book on bodies and embodiment or even interrogated my own story had I not entered into a deep relationship with Erin C. Law. She shows me a kind, quality, and texture of love that is deeply embodied and attuned to the healing I am in need of. I am a changed human because of my relationship with Erin and her love for me. She helps me be a better theologian and ethicist every day, and I am most happy in the mundane of life with them. My writing process has changed in that I am more attuned to my body and what is emerging within me. My work has changed because of Erin and because of their somatic wisdom. My life has changed because I now have a family, and Margot Law, Erin's mom, has become my chosen mother. You have the book that you have because Erin helped me tell my story in a way that is embodied and facilitates somatic wisdom. I hope they know how important their work is to me and to the world. I am so grateful that our paths have crossed and we have learned how to dance a dance that others might feel the pull to join!

Finally, I am grateful for Cara Arndorfer, who has been collaborating with me in therapy for many years. I first walked into her office in 2015 telling her I wanted to have a relationship with my body, and six years later, I wrote a book on my discoveries. Cara is a skilled therapist who helps me compost white body supremacy every week and invites me into a path of somatic and psychological healing, but I don't ever see myself arriving at a destination. I think my life's work is found along this path of healing, and I'm so grateful to have a conversation partner who values compassion and empathy and Queer relationality.

Books emerge by and through relationships. Many relationships have shaped me to create conditions for this book's emergence. While I cannot name every relationship that has shaped me, because there are literally hundreds of people who shape me and have shaped me throughout the years, I mentioned the primary ones who shape me on a daily basis. The majority of the relationships that shape me are with women or femme-identified persons, and it's important to name that because I am a Transmasculine person who is benefiting from the labor of women and femmes. I am grateful for this labor, and I remain grateful for the women and femmes who invest in me so that I might be the kind of generative scholar who invites more contemplation and conversation in the way of justice.